THE
PRAYER
OF
PROTECTION
DEVOTIONAL

ALSO BY JOSEPH PRINCE

For more information on these books and other inspiring resources, visit JosephPrince.com.

THE
PRAYER
OF
PROTECTION
DEVOTIONAL

JOSEPH PRINCE

Faith
Words

New York • Boston • Nashville

FaithWords
Hachette Book Group
1290 Avenue of the Americas
New York, NY 10104
faithwords.com
twitter.com/faithwords

First Edition: April 2017

FaithWords is a division of Hachette Book Group, Inc.
The FaithWords name and logo are trademarks of Hachette Book Group, Inc.

The publisher is not responsible for websites (or their content) that are not owned by the publisher.

The Hachette Speakers Bureau provides a wide range of authors for speaking events. To find out more, go to www.hachettespeakersbureau.com or call (866) 376-6591.

Literary development: Lance Wubbels Literary Services, Bloomington, Minnesota.

ISBN: 9781546006114 (Special edition)

Printed in the United States of America

Printing 1, 2023

CONTENTS

✣

Introduction

INTRODUCTION

We live in dangerous times. A time in which a person could be attacked by terrorists while watching a concert. A time during which an epidemic from one country could spread to another through a single traveler. A time when earthquakes, floods, and other calamities seem to be happening all too often. A time of violence, conflict, and wars.

Unfortunately, we already know that the world is going to get even darker. Isaiah 60:2 tells us this: *Darkness shall cover the earth, and deep darkness the people.*

But I have good news for you, my friend. Good news of the promises in God's Word that will fortify you and equip you during these times. Good news of His protection and His favor upon you. Good news that declares that you are *in* this world, but not *of* this world!

Isaiah 60:2 does not end with deep darkness. It goes on to declare this: *But the LORD will arise over you, and His glory will be seen upon you.*

The darker the world becomes, the brighter YOU will shine. As gloom and despair cover the earth, your light will become increasingly radiant. You will be His beacon of grace and glory in the midst of deep darkness. The world will see you walking in the fullness of the Lord's blessings and favor, and wonder how you and your household could be protected from the destruction and chaos all around.

You may be familiar with the Old Testament story of Daniel's friends, who were thrown into a fiery furnace for refusing to bow down to the golden idol of King Nebuchadnezzar. The king, his governors, and his counselors all witnessed for themselves how the fire had no power over the three Hebrew boys. Not a single strand of their hair was singed nor were their garments scorched. In fact, they walked away from the furnace without so much as the smell of smoke or fire on them!

Beloved, I want you to picture Daniel's friends walking out of that fiery furnace, completely unharmed. That's a picture of you and me today. In Christ, we are *in* this world, but we are not *of* this world. Even when thrown into the most extreme and challenging circumstances, we can walk out unharmed. The same Lord Jesus who stood with Shadrach, Meshach, and Abednego in the furnace stands with you today!

The darkness is real. The fire is real. The dangers in this world are certainly real, but His promise that you can live protected, untouched, and fearlessly can be an even greater reality in your life.

The Word of God tells us that fear involves torment. Our Father in heaven doesn't want any of His beloved children tormented by fear. His Word tells us, "There is no fear in love [dread does not exist], but full-grown (complete, perfect) love turns fear out of doors *and* expels every trace of terror!" (1 John 4:18 AMPC).

This collection of ninety daily devotionals contains excerpts from my original book, *The Prayer of Protection*, that will help anchor you in God's protective love for you and garrison your heart. Whatever fear it is that grips your heart, I want *every* trace of it to be expelled. You are not a hapless bystander who has no choice but to live in fear. No, you are set apart by your heavenly Abba. You are His beloved, and He who watches over you *never* slumbers or sleeps (see Ps. 121:4)! And yet, we cannot take His protection for granted.

The Prayer of Protection Devotional is divided into twelve sections. Each section uncovers what the Bible says about divine protection and provides faith-building truths that I know will strengthen you. The goal is for you to take just a brief amount of time each day to read and reflect, to see the circumstances in your life in the light of what you've learned in each reading, and to let God's promises of protection fill your heart, mind, and mouth.

Each of the daily readings was selected to show you how you can personally apply and learn to pray the prayer of protection found in Psalm 91. I've added several other features to help you apply and live out the truths that God wants you to know. Each daily devotional includes:

A key verse: A powerful, faith-building Scripture that relates to the inspirational reading, giving it a biblical foundation and anchoring your heart on divine protection. I encourage you to meditate on these daily Scriptures—you will be surprised how much the Holy Spirit will open up God's Word to you and refresh and strengthen your heart!

A devotional excerpt from *The Prayer of Protection*: An inspiring new covenant truth that ministers God's promises of protection, renews your mind, and releases you to experience freedom from every fear. These truths cover what it means to dwell in the secret place of the Most High God and the keys to living fearlessly in the protection of the Father's love. You will also see how the application of these truths has led believers to experience God's amazing protection firsthand.

Today's Prayer: A faith-filled prayer meant to help you express your heart to your heavenly Father. Feel free to adapt these prayers to your own situations. Just speak from your heart. Remember, the effective, fervent prayer of a child of God avails much (see James 5:16). Your Father is waiting and listening!

Today's Thought: A simple, powerful thought based on the daily reading and Scripture to help you focus on God's protection and His favor upon you. Let these thoughts guard your mind from any fear or defeatist thought that the enemy throws at you.

Our Lord is the same yesterday, today, and forever. In the same way He supernaturally delivered the precious individuals whose stories you will read in this book, He will deliver you too. As you put these promises on divine protection into action, you will experience miracles of deliverance, protection, and healing in your life.

These ninety readings should be read at a one-each-day pace so that they carry you through three months or so. It is my prayer that as you journey through the powerful revelations contained in this book, you will be empowered to truly live confidently and fearlessly in these dangerous times.

Psalm 91

He who dwells in the secret place of the Most High
Shall abide under the shadow of the Almighty.
I will say of the Lord, "*He is* my refuge and my fortress;
My God, in Him I will trust."

Surely He shall deliver you from the snare of the fowler
And from the perilous pestilence.
He shall cover you with His feathers,
And under His wings you shall take refuge;
His truth *shall be your* shield and buckler.
You shall not be afraid of the terror by night,
Nor of the arrow *that* flies by day,
Nor of the pestilence *that* walks in darkness,
Nor of the destruction *that* lays waste at noonday.

A thousand may fall at your side,
And ten thousand at your right hand;
But it shall not come near you.
Only with your eyes shall you look,
And see the reward of the wicked.

Because you have made the LORD, *who is* my refuge,
Even the Most High, your dwelling place,
No evil shall befall you,
Nor shall any plague come near your dwelling;
For He shall give His angels charge over you,
To keep you in all your ways.
In *their* hands they shall bear you up,
Lest you dash your foot against a stone.
You shall tread upon the lion and the cobra,
The young lion and the serpent you shall trample underfoot.

"Because he has set his love upon Me, therefore I will deliver him;
I will set him on high, because he has known My name.
He shall call upon Me, and I will answer him;
I *will be* with him in trouble;
I will deliver him and honor him.
With long life I will satisfy him,
And show him My salvation."

SECTION I

THE SECRET PLACE

He who dwells in the secret place of the Most High
Shall abide under the shadow of the Almighty.
—Psalm 91:1

SEATED WITH CHRIST

He who dwells in the secret place of the Most High
shall abide under the shadow of the Almighty.

—*Psalm 91:1*

There is a lot of fearmongering everywhere you turn today—on the news, in the papers, via social media, and unfortunately, on Christian media as well. However, it is vital that we do not let fear take over our hearts. As believers, we have no business feeding on fear. If your mind is entangled with knots of anxiety, perhaps it's time for you to examine your mental diet. What have you, consciously or unconsciously, been meditating on? Are you ingesting and believing everything you see in the news reports, or are you living by what the Lord Jesus has purchased for you at Calvary?

To help you understand God's heart for you regarding fear and your walking in His protection, I want to share with you a powerful key from today's verse, the very first verse of Psalm 91, the prayer of protection. The Hebrew word for "dwell" is *yashab*, which means to *sit down*, to remain, or to settle.[1] Notice that the very first thing that God wants you to do to enjoy His protection is to *rest*. His protection, peace, love, and other blessings flow in your life when you are in a place of rest.

Let's camp on the word *dwell* just a little more. Let's meditate on what it means to rest or "sit down." The Bible says that we are *seated with Christ* at God's right hand (see Eph. 2:6, Heb. 1:3). The word "seated" is beautiful—it means that you are no longer standing and working.

Under the old covenant, the priest had to offer the morning sacrifice at 9 a.m., and then remain standing for six hours until after the evening sacrifice at 3 p.m. Our Lord Jesus was crucified at 9 a.m. and He hung on the cross for six hours until He died at 3 p.m., thus fulfilling the type of both the morning and evening sacrifices (see Heb. 10:11–12). Because Jesus became the final sacrifice, the work of the priest is done and he no longer has to stand. Because our Lord cried, "It is finished!" at Calvary (John 19:30), we are today *seated* in Christ. We can dwell in the secret place of the Most High—a place of peace, safety, and security—*and* we can live fear-free because the blood of our Lord Jesus has paid for every blessing of protection in Psalm 91!

Today, whether you are dealing with a difficult financial situation, a sleep disorder, or plagued by depressive or even suicidal thoughts, my desire is for you to discover a God who loves you, and whose strong hands of protection are over your entire life and over every area that concerns you.

Today's Prayer
Father, thank You for the great love with which You have loved me and made me to sit with Jesus at Your right hand. I gladly choose to enter into the rest found only in the finished work of Your Son and to dwell in Your secret place of peace, safety, and security. I believe I can live fear-free today because of the blood of Jesus. Amen.

Today's Thought
Because of the blood of Jesus, I am in the secret place of the Most High, divinely protected and able to live fearlessly.

THE POWERFUL NAMES OF GOD

The name of the LORD is a strong tower;
the righteous run to it and are safe.

—*Proverbs 18:10*

In the last reading, we learned that because of the completed work of our Lord Jesus, we can dwell "in the secret place of the Most High," having free access into the presence of our *Elyon*, the Most High. We can "abide under the shadow of the Almighty," or *Shaddai*. These two Hebrew names of God—*Elyon* and *Shaddai*—in the first verse of Psalm 91 alone help to put our problems in perspective, don't they? In and of ourselves, our present challenges may appear insurmountable. But when we are resting in the presence of *El Elyon*—God Most High, the possessor of heaven and earth (see Gen. 14:19)—and abiding under the shadow of *El Shaddai*—God Almighty, the all-sufficient One—all of a sudden, our adversities don't seem so intimidating after all!

My prayer for you is that your perspective of God will be enlarged as you see Him and His attributes in the Scriptures and discover the power of His living Word, as Carina from North Carolina did:

My grandson, Caylen, was born three months premature, weighing 1lb 7oz. He was in the hospital for almost six months. We were told that his survival rate was low. Even if he did survive, he would have significant development delays.

At the time of his hospitalization, his mother was asked if there was a Bible verse that she wanted to be placed above her son's incubator. She gave them Psalm 91. I don't know if my daughter had any idea of the power of putting that psalm above his incubator. I did not realize how powerful it was until later.

Caylen had surgery for his heart and also two more for his stomach. He did well in all his surgeries, so much so that the doctor commented, "I don't think he realizes he is supposed to be sick."

My grandson is now six years old with no developmental delays and advanced in almost every area. Praise the Lord!

God took little Caylen into that secret place where he was safe and received healing. I saw firsthand how the world could not harm him and he is now a walking testimony of the power and love of God.

My friend, there is no doubt that there is power in the Word of God. There is healing power in the prayer of protection! I pray that you'll also let His Word strengthen you and cause you to rest in the protection and might of our *El Elyon* and *El Shaddai*.

Today's Prayer

Father, thank You that I can run to You and find strength in You. I commit all my concerns into Your hands. I thank You for Your abiding presence with me and I rest in Your love, protection, and might. Amen.

Today's Thought

I will rest in the presence of El Elyon—*God Most High, the possessor of heaven and earth—and abide under the shadow of* El Shaddai—*God Almighty, the all-sufficient One—whose power no foe can withstand!*

WHERE IS THIS SECRET PLACE?

*For as many as are the promises of God, they all find their
Yes [answer] in Him [Christ]. For this reason we also
utter the Amen (so be it) to God through Him [in His
Person and by His agency] to the glory of God.*
—*2 Corinthians 1:20* AMPC

Where is this secret place of the Most High and how do you get there? Before I answer this question, I want you to be careful of preaching and teaching about Psalm 91 that make "the secret place of the Most High" a place that only an elite few can go to, while the rest of us have no access to it because we haven't done enough, such as pray for eight hours. Usually, the person who teaches along these lines is trying to say that there is a standard of holiness that you must attain before you can reach the secret place of the Most High. Now, if this is true and it takes eight hours of prayer at home to be in the secret place of the Most High, then how about those of us who have full-time jobs and can't pray for eight hours, and who really need protection?

Think about it for a moment. Who needs more protection—the one praying in the safety of his home or the one working out there? Clearly, it is the guy who is working out there in the world where accidents are possible and where he is exposed to all kinds of viruses. Yet, according to this teaching, he cannot access the secret place because he has not prayed eight hours a day! Does this even make sense to you? That's why I don't like teaching that makes certain people—especially the preacher—appear like they are part of an elite few. The Lord's blessings are not just for an elite few. If a blessing is from our Lord, *everyone* has access to it. The young and the old, the strong and the weak, the rich and the poor—*all* have access by faith to His blessings that are freely given.

Let me tell you where the secret place of the Most High is. The secret place of the Most High is a place where you are *in Christ*. Wouldn't you agree that being in Christ is to be in the safest hiding place? How did you get to be in Christ? By receiving the Lord Jesus as your personal Lord and Savior. Once you are a born-again believer, our heavenly Father sees you in Christ. You are safe, protected, and secure in *the* hiding place! Be anchored in this truth and see yourself walking in a greater measure of His divine protection in the days to come.

Today's Prayer

Father God, thank You that being in the secret place of the Most High is my reality. I anchor my life on Your Word that tells me You have brought me into this secret place in our Lord Jesus. I believe that in Christ, I am in the safest hiding place I can ever be, and that every promise of protection in Your Word is Yes and Amen for me. Amen.

Today's Thought

As a born-again believer, I am safe, protected, and secure in Christ, my hiding place, where every promise of protection found in His Word is Yes and Amen for me.

SAFE IN THE ARK

*Then the L*ORD *said to Noah, "Come into the ark,
you and all your household, because I have seen that
you are righteous before Me in this generation."*

—*Genesis 7:1*

~⚜~

Remember how Noah was safe in the ark when the flood-waters came? While Noah was not perfect, God saw him as righteous because of his faith in God (see Heb. 11:7). When the flood came, everyone outside the ark died, but Noah and his family were protected and saved. Why? Because they were in the ark, which is a type of Christ, who is our salvation (see Acts 4:12).

The ark didn't have windows along its sides, only near the roof. The truth here is that God does not want you to focus on all the darkness, terror, and evil that are around you and in the world. He wants you to look up and know that His Son is coming back for you. I want you to see something else: I believe there were times when Noah might have lost his balance and fallen as the storm waters crashed against the ark. But Noah fell *in* the ark; he never fell *out* of the ark.

Similarly, for the believer today, when the devil tempts you and you fall, you don't fall out of your position in Christ; you are still *in* Christ. In the book of Proverbs, it says, "For a righteous *man* may fall seven times and rise again" (Prov. 24:16). You see, a believer doesn't fall in and out of righteousness. Our righteousness today is a gift from our Lord Jesus Christ (see Rom. 5:17). This means that even though we may fail from time to time because we are imperfect human beings, we are still in Christ our ark and do not forfeit His blessings of protection.

Now, in case you are wondering, does this make someone want to live recklessly? Certainly not! I believe that knowing you are righteous in Christ makes you live responsibly and in honor to the Lord (see Rom. 6:10–14). The revelation of our righteousness in Christ produces righteous living (see Titus 2:11–12).

Today's Prayer

*Lord Jesus, thank You that You alone are the ark
of my salvation. Thank You that the Father sees me as
righteous because my faith is in You. Thank You for giving
me Your righteousness as a gift. I believe that even
when I fail, I am still in You and Your blessings of
protection are still mine. Amen.*

Today's Thought

*As an imperfect human being, I may fail from time
to time. But I am still in Christ my ark and do not
forfeit His blessings of protection.*

DAY 5

VALUING WHAT YOU HAVE IN CHRIST

*To them God willed to make known what are the riches
of the glory of this mystery among the Gentiles: which is
Christ in you, the hope of glory.*

—*Colossians 1:27*

My dear reader, the more you grow in your revelation and valuation of how Jesus' finished work has placed you in Him—in the secret place where you are safe, protected, and secure—the more you'll find your heart at rest instead of filled with worry and fears. Something powerful happens in your heart and in your outward circumstances when you begin to value being in Christ, in the secret place of the Father's care, protection, and love.

Let me give you an illustration of what it means to value something. Suppose I brought you an old, dusty violin with two missing strings and I said to you, "Isn't this beautiful?" Your reaction would probably be, "That's not beautiful; that's old and worthless." But if I told you it's an original Stradivarius that used to belong to a world-famous violinist, all of a sudden, your appreciation of this dusty, old violin would swell and you'd ask if you could hold it. What happened? Your appreciation of the violin changed when you understood its true value.

In the same way, I want to encourage you to value the preciousness of what it means to be in Christ—being in the secret place of inseparable closeness with Him, where we have His loving presence constantly with us, watching over us and protecting us. I strongly encourage you to keep hearing anointed preaching that keeps revealing who you are and what you have in Christ. Keep hearing grace-based teachings on God's promises to protect you, as well as praise reports of God's grace and protection over His people. Why? Because as you do, you'll begin to value being in the secret place more and more. As you do, you'll find your heart and mind more and more at rest in Him. You'll wake up every morning confident of His tender care, protection, and preservation. You'll live life full of hope and zest instead of worry and fear, and see Him deliver and protect you from whatever the enemy may throw at you!

Today's Prayer
*Abba, Father, thank You that Your Word shows me
the riches of being in Christ Jesus, the hope of glory.
Thank You for bringing me into this secret place of
inseparable closeness to Him, where His loving presence
is constantly with me. I rest in His tender care,
protection, and preservation. Amen.*

Today's Thought
*Because I am in Christ, I am in the secret place of my
Savior's care, protection, and love—all the time.*

DESIRING SPIRITUAL INTIMACY

"You shall dwell in the land of Goshen, and you shall be near to me, you and your children, your children's children, your flocks and your herds, and all that you have. There I will provide for you, lest you and your household, and all that you have, come to poverty; for there are still five years of famine."

—*Genesis 45:10–11*

The "secret place" speaks of a place *in Christ*, but it also speaks of intimacy. To be "under the shadow of the Almighty" is to be close to Him. There are times when I travel to Israel with my pastors and the sun is scorching hot. When we are outdoors, whether it is on the Mount of Beatitudes or in Capernaum, we always look forward to being under the shadow of a tree. The difference in temperature when we are under the protective shelter of a tree is like night and day. Out in the open, we wouldn't last long under the scorching heat of the sun. But under the shadow of a tree, we can sit for hours, enjoying a time of refreshing as we discuss the Word of God.

Beloved, being under the shadow of the Almighty speaks

of closeness, intimacy, and protection. It speaks of a place of refreshing, coolness, and rest. When Psalm 91 talks about dwelling in the "secret place" of the Most High, that secret place is not a geographical location, but *spiritual intimacy* with our Lord Jesus. In the same way, the prayer of protection is not an incantation or some kind of magic chant that grants you protection. It is you valuing your position in Christ and your close relationship with Him, and being found in that secret place with Him.

For more than a decade now, I have been teaching my church to declare Psalm 91 over themselves and their loved ones and to be conscious of the close relationship we as believers have with our Lord Jesus. Some years ago, I received a testimony of divine protection from a businessman who attended our church. He had been on a business trip and was staying at the Marriott Hotel in Jakarta, Indonesia. While he was in the lobby of the hotel, a bomb was detonated right outside and it tore through the lobby. The blast was so powerful that he saw a body flying past him. After the dust had settled, he realized that although his shirt was splattered with blood, and debris was strewn all around him, he was completely unharmed. Amazingly, he had stepped behind a pillar at the *very* moment the bomb went off, and that pillar had shielded him from the direct impact of the explosion.

Just think of what could have happened if this man had not reached the pillar at the precise second the bomb went off. All praise and glory to our Lord Jesus who watches over His own!

Today's Prayer
Abba, Father, thank You that though I am in a world that is getting darker, You have brought me near to You. Thank You that You have brought me to dwell in Your shadow, in the place of intimacy with You through my righteous standing in Christ Jesus. I believe that in this place of nearness, I am safe and sheltered and have nothing to fear. Amen.

Today's Thought
Because my Lord Jesus loves me, He is watching over and watching out for my loved ones and me today.

GOD'S ETERNAL, UNSHAKABLE WORD

And we desire that each one of you show the same
diligence to the full assurance of hope until the end,
that you do not become sluggish, but imitate those who
through faith and patience inherit the promises.

—Hebrews 6:11–12

⚭

The Lord has put a *now* word in my heart for the times we are living in, and that word is "protection." I want to show you from the Bible what Jesus died to give you in the area of protection. Even as I write this book, the Lord is commissioning me to preach strongly from Psalm 91 so that you can walk in His divine protection in these last days. Psalm 91 has just sixteen verses, but is loaded with many potent promises that we can stand upon.

Unfortunately, when we are faced with problems, whether it is a sickness, an accident, or any kind of trouble, many of us don't lay hold of and claim the Lord's deliverance found in His Word. Yet, when you do hold on to God's Word for deliverance, the devil is so afraid that the Word will become firmly rooted in your heart. That is why he will come immediately to try to steal the Word from your heart. He will point to your outward circumstances and taunt you with thoughts such as, "Look, your child is still sick—where is God now? Where is the reality of Psalm 91?" At that very moment, you are presented with a choice. You can either back away from God's Word and agree with the enemy, or you can stand in faith and continue to believe His promises.

Even as the Lord put it on my heart to write this book on divine protection, He told me that there are people reading this who might think, *I have claimed the promises in Psalm 91 before and it didn't work.* My dear friend, I want to encourage you to hold on to His Word. Whatever your experience has been, the Word of God stands eternal and unshakable. If you have not experienced full protection in the past, I believe that as you hold on to His Word and persevere in faith, you will walk more and more in the Lord's total protection.

Today's Prayer

*Father, thank You for giving me Your eternal, unshakable
Word to study and be rooted in. I ask You to open my
eyes to Your many powerful promises and to keep my eyes
on Your unfailing grace and faithfulness. I believe that as
I continue to believe Your promises, I will walk more
and more in Your total protection. Amen.*

Today's Thought

*I believe the Word of God which says, "As for God, His way
is perfect; the word of the Lord is proven; He is a shield to
all who trust in Him" (Ps. 18:30).*

BUILD YOUR FAITH UPON HIS PROMISES

*"He shall deliver you in six troubles, yes, in seven no evil
shall touch you. In famine He shall redeem you from
death, and in war from the power of the sword. You shall
be hidden from the scourge of the tongue, and you shall
not be afraid of destruction when it comes. You shall
laugh at destruction and famine."*

—*Job 5:19–22*

I believe the Lord gave me the above portion of Scripture
to strengthen you. Let's take a closer look at the first verse:
"He shall deliver you in six troubles, yes, in seven no evil shall
touch you." Now, I have read this verse a number of times
before, but the Lord quickened this Scripture in me, so let me
share this fresh insight with you. I want to specially address
those who have been greatly discouraged in the area of protection. Perhaps you have experienced a very difficult or even
tragic event, or are going through a very challenging situation
right now. Can I encourage you to build your faith upon His
promises and not upon your experiences?

The Word of God says that in this world, we will have trouble (see John 16:33). The fact that God declares in His Word that He will deliver us from troubles tells us that we will experience troubles. But God wants us to know that the more we hear preaching on Psalm 91, the more we quote it and remind ourselves of the Lord's protection daily, the more our faith in His protection will grow.

Faith comes from "hearing, and hearing by the word of Christ" (Rom. 10:17 NASB). The more we hear, the more we believe! The more we claim and pray the prayer of protection, the more we will walk in its blessings. That is the intention of this book—to saturate you with the hearing and hearing of the Lord's protection promises for your life until your faith is robust and overflowing.

My dear reader, deliverance from trouble is fantastic, but there is a promise that is even greater, and that is when you are at that place where "no evil shall touch you." That's my prayer for you and your loved ones. While we live in dangerous times, we have an almighty God who watches over us. May we all increase and have a progressive revelation of the Lord's protection in these last days. While none of us, myself included, are there yet, we are on a journey of faith, of walking fully in the promises of God's protection. Let's give thanks to the Lord for His deliverance from all our troubles as we continue to believe we will come to the place where no evil will touch our loved ones and us!

Today's Prayer

Lord Jesus, thank You that You are with me on this journey of faith, and encouraging me with Your promises of protection. Thank You that I can build my faith upon Your Word and not my experiences. I believe that the more I claim and pray the prayer of protection, the more I will walk in all its blessings. Amen.

Today's Thought

The more I believe and am conscious of the Lord's protection daily, the more I will experience deliverance from trouble after trouble until I come to a place where no evil will touch me.

SECTION II

"I WILL SAY"

I will say of the LORD, "He is my refuge and my fortress;
My God, in Him I will trust."

—*Psalm 91:2*

DAY 1

YOUR REFUGE AND FORTRESS

I will say of the Lord, "He is my refuge and my fortress;
my God, in Him I will trust."

—Psalm 91:2

What are you saying of the Lord today? If you are saying He gave you the trouble you are presently in or an illness to teach you humility, it's time to change what you believe about Him. If you really believe that God is the author of your problems, would you really be running to Him for help?

My friend, let's be like the psalmist who declared, "I will **say** of the Lord, '*He is* my refuge and my fortress; my God, in Him I will trust'" (boldface mine).

The Hebrew word for "refuge," *machaceh*, refers to a shelter from storms and danger.[2] This shelter is like the bunkers that many Jews have in their homes in Israel today to shelter them from small-scale attacks. In the figurative sense, when you say the Lord is your *machaceh*, you are also declaring that He is your place of hope.

The Lord is also your fortress. In Hebrew, the word used

for "fortress" is *matsuwd*. It refers to a castle or stronghold,[3] a place of defense and protection against large-scale attacks. Isn't that a beautiful picture? Whatever you might be going through right now, you can declare that the Lord is your refuge and your fortress—your protection in both small as well as big attacks.

Perhaps you have not been saying that God is behind your troubles. Perhaps you are not saying *anything* about the Lord at all. Perhaps God seems far away and you feel cut off from Him. If that is you, can I encourage you to take a break today from whatever you have on your busy to-do list, and simply take time to dwell in His sweet presence? God is not distant; sometimes we are just too distracted to hear His voice or sense His loving presence.

Take a moment and see yourself in His secret place. Abide under His shadow. Savor His favor. Receive His wisdom. And find rest for your troubled soul. The feeling of being distant from God is only a feeling, nothing more. He has promised in His Word that He will never leave you nor forsake you (see Heb. 13:5). Our Lord Jesus paid for you to have access to God's constant presence. At the cross, He cried out, "My God, My God, why have You forsaken Me?" when God turned His back on Him (Matt. 27:46). He took our place and was rejected by God when He carried our sins so that today, we can take His place of being in the constant presence of the Father and take Him as our refuge and fortress.

––––––––––

Today's Prayer
Lord Jesus, thank You that You are my refuge and my fortress, my shelter from storms and dangers, and my stronghold against small and big attacks. I come under Your shadow to be covered by Your favor, receive Your wisdom, and find rest for my soul. I believe that because of Your finished work on the cross, I can always dwell in Your sweet presence and experience Your protection. Amen.

Today's Thought
I declare that the Lord is my refuge and my fortress, my shelter from all danger, and my place of hope!

EXPERIENCE HIS PRESENCE

Yes, though I walk through the [deep, sunless] valley
of the shadow of death, I will fear or dread no evil,
for You are with me; Your rod [to protect] and
Your staff [to guide], they comfort me.

—*Psalm 23:4* AMPC

My dear reader, today you can experience God's presence in your life. Say to yourself, "The Lord is with me and I have His favor, blessings, and protection." Sense His shadow covering you. His shadow is a picture of nearness. You are not trying to get into the secret place; you are *already* there in Christ. In Christ, you can't get any closer to God. In the Old Testament, God showed Moses, the great patriarch, only His back parts (see Ex. 33:22–23). That's the old covenant—because of man's failure, God was always departing and the children of Israel only saw His back.

The picture of the new covenant is God sending His only Son, Jesus Christ. It is the picture of the father running toward the prodigal son in spite of his failures. Under the new covenant, we are seated with our heavenly Father in Christ and we see the smile on His face! That is how close you are to God today. So even if your feelings tell you that God is a million miles away, learn to trust His Word over your feelings. All you need to do is to utter the words "Father" or "Abba," and immediately you will sense that He is closer than your own breath.

In the same way, even when you don't seem to feel His presence, you can trust in Him. Trust doesn't mean that there will be no butterflies in your stomach. Trust means that even though you have the butterflies, you still act on God's Word. Whatever it is you are afraid of doing, do it afraid while keeping your trust in the Lord. There are people who are afraid to leave their house, fly on a plane, pursue a new career, start a new friendship, volunteer in a ministry, visit a care group in church, or even show up for work.

Beloved, don't let fear rule your life. If you're thinking of embarking on something, most certainly, be led by the Spirit, seek wise counsel, count the cost, and make responsible decisions in your situation. Just don't allow the butterflies in your stomach to dictate your life. When you say to the Lord, "In You I trust," it doesn't mean you instantly stop feeling any fear. Trust means choosing to act on God's Word in spite of the fear.

Today's Prayer

Daddy God, thank You that I can come to You and cry out, "Abba," and immediately sense Your presence and love for me. Thank You that even when I don't seem to feel Your presence, I can trust in You, and draw on Your peace and Your strength. I believe that You are always with me and I can choose to act on Your Word in the face of every fear. Amen.

Today's Thought

The Lord Himself has said, "I will never leave you nor forsake you." So I can boldly say, "The Lord is my helper; I will not fear" (Heb. 13:5–6).

SECRETS OF PROTECTION IN THE NAMES OF GOD

The LORD also will be a refuge for the oppressed,
a refuge in times of trouble. And those who know
Your name will put their trust in You; for You, LORD,
have not forsaken those who seek You.

—Psalm 9:9–10

In the previous section, I mentioned how we find two names of God in the first verse of Psalm 91 and how that brings comfort and strength to us when we feel afraid or weak. Each of the names of God has a divine attribute, and understanding and believing that He is each attribute will cause that attribute to flow into our lives. The first name of God mentioned in Psalm 91 is "Most High" (*Elyon*), which means He is the Most High God and there is no one higher than Him. He is the possessor of heaven and earth (see Gen. 14:19). The verse goes on to refer to God as the "Almighty." In Hebrew, it is *Shaddai*—the God who blesses you with more than enough, more than you can contain. Man has limitations but we have a God who is abundantly unlimited.

Now, the second verse of Psalm 91 contains another two names of God. Isn't this so powerful? When the psalmist declares, "I will say of the LORD," he is referring to *Yehovah* or *Yahweh*, the covenant-keeping God.[4] It is the holiest name of the Lord, the name Jewish scribes treat with great reverence.

Do you know that Jesus' name in Hebrew, *Yeshua*, actually means "*Yahweh* saves"?[5] It is not "*Yahweh* judges." The name *Jesus* means "*Yahweh* SAVES." If you are broke, *Yahweh* saves. If you are sick, *Yahweh* saves. If you have enemies that are coming against you, *Yahweh* saves. Whatever saving you need, Jesus is the answer, for His name means "*Yahweh* saves." Hallelujah!

The psalmist in verse 2 goes on to say, "My God, in Him I will trust." Now, the word "God" here refers to *Elohim*, the God of power, the Creator.[6] The God who created the heavens and the earth (see Gen. 1:1). This is our God! He is the One we put our trust in.

In just two verses, you find four names of God mentioned. Knowing, believing, and saying He is all these to us gives us protection in our everyday situations. He will deliver and rescue the one who knows His name. Hallelujah!

Today's Prayer

Abba, Father, thank You for revealing Your precious names to me. Thank You that You are Elyon, *the Most High;* Shaddai, *the Almighty;* Yahweh, *the covenant-keeping God; and* Elohim, *the God of power, the Creator. Thank You for the most loving and powerful name of all,* Jesus. *I believe that* Jesus *is my Lord and Savior for every need, and I put my trust in Him. Amen.*

Today's Thought

According to the Word, I will declare that my God saves me: "He who dwells in the secret place of Elyon *shall abide under the shadow of* Shaddai. *I will say of* Yahweh, 'He is *my refuge and my fortress; my* Elohim, *in Him I will trust'" (Ps. 91:1–2).*

BELIEVE WITH YOUR HEART

*For indeed the gospel was preached to us as
well as to them; but the word which they heard
did not profit them, not being mixed with
faith in those who heard it.*

—*Hebrews 4:2*

Jennifer from Taiwan shared this powerful praise report with me that demonstrates the power of *actively listening* to messages on Psalm 91. By active listening, I mean she did exactly what the verse above describes. As she listened to the promises of Psalm 91, she mixed what she was hearing with her faith to the point that she began to share the psalm with her family members and declare the power of God's protection over them. Look at what she shared:

> I am from Taiwan but I live in Singapore, and for more than a year, I have been attending New Creation Church. When Pastor Prince started preaching strongly on Psalm 91 in 2014, I began meditating on the verses. I also began sharing the psalm with my family back

home in Kaohsiung, Taiwan, and declaring it over my family members.

On July 26 of that year, my brother, Daniel, got into a car accident and was badly injured. When my mother called and told me he was lying unconscious in the emergency room, I told her that Daniel would be fine because the Lord has promised to deliver us from trouble. My mother and I also took the Holy Communion on his behalf and prayed for him. I had a strong sense of peace and was not worried.

The next day my brother regained consciousness, and the doctor said he was extremely "lucky" that his brain and internal organs were all intact. After he completed all his surgeries and treatments, the hospital informed my mom that Daniel, who was heavily bandaged and still in pain, had to give up his bed for more seriously sick people. Though this was very upsetting, my brother was brought home and my mom and sister took turns to care for him. I told my mom then that Daniel would be fine because our heavenly Father would take care of him. We also declared Psalm 91 together.

The next day, July 31, a series of gas explosions in Kaohsiung ripped apart city streets across three districts, including the one where my mom's house is located.

However, her house was untouched as the effect of the explosions and damages they caused stopped just a few blocks away. Thank God that Daniel was sent home to be cared for—my family could stay by his side and did not have to travel to the hospital and experience all the chaos out there in the streets. Also, with all the casualties from the gas explosion, it would have meant little rest and care for Daniel in the hospital, as there were simply too many patients.

My brother has experienced a supernatural healing and is recovering very well now. Interestingly, he has a red, heart-shaped wound on his leg. My brother himself says that instead of being reminded of the pain and fear from the car accident, the wound reminds him of the love, healing, and restoration of his heavenly Father every day.

We thank God for His supernatural protection and deliverance. He has not only delivered Daniel from the accident, but also protected my whole family from the gas explosion. A lot of things could have happened but the Lord took care of them all! We thank God that He is faithful and we thank Him for Pastor Prince's ministry.

Many people heard me preach on the prayer of protection, but you can tell that Jennifer ran with the teaching. I pray that as you "listen" to the words in this book, you are coming alive and mixing your faith with the promises of Psalm 91 as Jennifer did.

Believing begins on the inside. Faith begins on the inside. When the Word of God is preached, faith is the hand that takes. Faith says, "That's mine! The promises of God's protection are *mine*!" What begins inside is then reinforced outside—you begin to speak the Word out loud.

Today's Prayer

Heavenly Father, thank You for showing me how I can mix my faith with the promises of protection in Psalm 91. Thank You that Your Spirit in me is causing me to come alive as I actively listen to Your Word, meditate on it, and speak it over myself, my loved ones, and even others. Faith is arising in me and I boldly declare, "The promises of Your protection are mine!" Amen.

Today's Thought

I am actively listening to the promises of Psalm 91 and mixing them with my faith. By faith I declare that the promises of God's protection are mine!

SPEAKING OUT IN FAITH

*And since we have the same spirit of faith, according to what is written, "I **believed** and therefore I **spoke**," we also **believe** and therefore **speak**.*

—*2 Corinthians 4:13 (boldface mine)*

Having read what I've said about declaring God's promises of protection over yourself and your loved ones, you may be asking, *But Pastor Prince, can't I just believe God's Word* in *my heart? Why do I also have to say Psalm 91 out loud?*

Let me show you some Scriptures about faith and speaking that will help you. Romans 10:9 tells us that "if you **confess** with your **mouth** the Lord Jesus and **believe** in your heart that God has raised Him from the dead, you will be saved" (boldface mine). Our Lord Jesus also said, "Whoever **says** to this mountain, 'Be removed and be cast into the sea,' and does not doubt in his heart, but **believes** that those things he **says** will be done, he will have whatever he **says**" (Mark 11:23, boldface mine).

Now, reread what the apostle Paul wrote in today's verse. Do you notice a pattern here? Faith involves *believing* in your heart as well as *speaking* with your mouth. You and I, we are made in God's image. When God first saw darkness, He didn't say, "Gosh, it's so dark." What did God do? He called forth light by speaking. He said, "Let there be light" (Gen. 1:3). In the New Testament, our Lord Jesus *spoke* to the storm and it subsided. He *spoke* to the fig tree and it withered. He *spoke* to the demons and they fled. He *spoke* to the sick and they were healed. He *spoke* to the dead and they lived.

Similarly, when we are faced with darkness in any area of our lives today, or trapped in a storm of challenges, let's not be mired in looking at the problems and despairing. We should also call forth what we want to see! If we find ourselves caught in a dangerous situation, we should declare, "The Lord is my refuge and my fortress." If there is a sickness in our body, we can call forth our healing by saying, "Thank You, Jesus, by Your stripes I am healed!" Start speaking forth your protection, your health, and your victory today!

Today's Prayer

Father God, thank You that my protection, health, and victory today are all about right believing and speaking Your Word into my situations. Help me to open my mouth and speak words that release my faith and Your power into those situations. I believe that I am created in Your image and that as You spoke light into existence, I can also call forth what I want to see and walk in the protection and victory my Lord Jesus has purchased for me. Amen.

Today's Thought

I will speak God's Word because this has the power to change my life and my situations.

THE POWER OF PRAYING AND SPEAKING PSALM 91

*So shall My word be that goes forth out of My mouth:
it shall not return to Me void [without producing
any effect, useless], but it shall accomplish that
which I please and purpose, and it shall prosper
in the thing for which I sent it.*

—Isaiah 55:11 AMPC

Let me now encourage you with another praise report of the power of praying and speaking Psalm 91 over our loved ones. This came from Brenda, who lives in Connecticut:

My twenty-four-year-old son, Lee, was crossing the street on a crosswalk in New York City when he was struck by a cab on the leg and thrown onto the hood of the car before landing on the street. Miraculously, he was totally fine after the accident! He did not have a single broken bone, bruise, or even a scratch.

I recall that just a few days before the accident, we were having a wonderful time celebrating Thanksgiving. Suddenly, I saw in my mind an image of Lee on a slab and dead in a morgue. I immediately dismissed that image, proclaimed that my son would live and not die, and pleaded the blood of Jesus over him.

I didn't tell anyone what I'd seen, but just thanked God for His protection for my son and all my family members in Jesus' name. The morning of Lee's accident, I also felt led to pray God's protection over my children from car accidents—not something that I usually do.

Then, later that afternoon, I received a text from Lee telling me about the accident and that he was unharmed. After hearing my son was fine, I got on my knees and cried tears of joy, thanking my wonderful Father God! I am so thankful that the Holy Spirit warned me before the accident happened so I could pray for his protection.

My son had just been awarded an awesome position in his company and we were all celebrating his wonderful new title and how God had opened up doors of favor for him. The accident happened just one day before he started his new job.

At the time I learned about Lee's accident, I was just listening to Joseph Prince's message on Psalm 91. I used to pray it over my family all the time, but over the years, I had forgotten about this powerful psalm. I *am thankful to Joseph Prince for reminding me of the power of Psalm 91. When we pray the Word of God over our children or any situation, we release His angels to work on our behalf.*

Our God is such a good God, isn't He? I trust that you are beginning to see how important it is to invest your time in getting His living and powerful Word into your heart, praying it over yourself and your loved ones, and speaking it out loud.

––––––––

Today's Prayer

Father, thank You that because of the blood of Your Son, Jesus, I am clothed in Your righteousness and the enemy has been defeated. I want Your Word to get deep inside my heart and to guard my heart in good and bad times. Help me to speak Your Word of divine protection over all the situations in my life. I believe You will cause my loved ones and me to reign over any attack or anything that comes against us. Amen.

Today's Thought

I reign in life over the enemy through the blood of the Lamb of God and the power of the spoken Word of God.

BUILD A SHIELD OF FAITH

Every word of God is tried and purified; He is a shield
to those who trust and take refuge in Him.
—*Proverbs 30:5* AMPC

❦

In the last reading, you'll note that Brenda was actively filling herself up with the promises of God's protection. When the Lord gave her a vision of her son being in danger, her heart was already full of faith (not fear) and she *spoke* out with authority against the evil coming against her son. When she heard about her son's accident, she was listening to preaching on Psalm 91. Coincidence? I think not. She was already building a shield of faith around her heart. Faith comes by hearing and hearing the word of Christ (see Rom. 10:17 NASB).

What are you hearing today? The word of the world? The word of Wall Street? Or the word of Christ?

I want to encourage you today to build a shield of faith around your family. Listen, believe, speak. Would you say it with me? Listen, believe, speak. Listen to Christ-centered messages, believe the Word of God, and speak out loud the promises you want to see in your life.

I believe that the Lord wants to seal this truth in your life today. Say this out loud with me right now:

Lord Jesus, You are our family's refuge, our fortress, our God—in You we trust. We don't trust in our own wisdom, our own limited intelligence, and our own abilities. We trust in You. We trust in Your grace and Your love for us. We trust You to keep us in Your divine health and strength all the days of our lives. We trust You to keep us from terror, from fear, from dangers, from disease, and from accidents. In You we trust. Amen.

64

Today's Prayer
Abba, Father, thank You that no matter what the enemy brings against me, You have given me faith as a mighty shield to overcome them all. Thank You for the precious word of Christ that I can believe and declare to see Your promises manifest in my life. By faith I declare that I already have the victory over every one of the enemy's attacks. Amen.

Today's Thought
Today I stand upon the unshakable foundation of the word of Christ and speak the promises of God. No plague, no death, no harm, and no evil can come near me because my Lord Jesus has paid the full penalty for my sins and for me to receive His divine protection.

RIGHT PLACE, RIGHT TIME

*Surely He shall deliver you from the snare of the fowler
And from the perilous pestilence.*

—Psalm 91:3

WE ARE IN THIS WORLD BUT NOT OF THIS WORLD

Surely He shall deliver you from the snare of the fowler
and from the perilous pestilence.

—*Psalm 91:3*

❧

Surely He *shall* deliver you from the snare of the fowler. Not "maybe" or "sometimes," but an unqualified "surely." Not a conditional "He *might*" but a definitive "He *shall*." What blessed assurance we have that our God *will* deliver us from the snare of the fowler!

The Bible depicts the devil as a fowler. A fowler is a professional bird catcher. He lays traps and carefully conceals them so that he can ambush unsuspecting birds. The Bible also depicts the devil as a thief and murderer who comes to steal, kill, and destroy (see John 10:10).

What we need to understand is that the world we live in is a fallen world. Adam committed high treason and gave the keys of this world to the devil. Because of what Adam did, the devil is the ruler of this world. The apostle Paul calls him "the prince of the power of the air" (Eph. 2:2). That is why as long as the devil is still the ruler of this world, the world will continue to get darker and darker and there will continue to be accidents, sicknesses, calamities, tragedies, and deaths.

But we can rejoice in the knowledge that the devil's lease on this world is quickly running out. Apostle Paul also tells us that our Lord Jesus is coming back and all His enemies will be humbled or put under His feet, with death as the last enemy to be destroyed (see 1 Cor. 15:26).

In the meantime, we will see the world getting darker and darker. But as believers, we do not need to live in fear. Our trust is in our Lord Jesus. We are *in* this world, but we are not *of* this world (see John 17:16). There is a very real and active fowler that is setting up snares. Even as I write this book, I'm reading and hearing reports of bombs going off, shootings, a commercial airplane crashing upon landing, and viral outbreaks in different parts of the world.

In the natural, this can be extremely disheartening. But don't forget that we have a Savior who is even more real, and He has promised to deliver us from the snare of the fowler and from perilous pestilences (dangerous diseases and viruses). The bottom-line is, we need to realize how much we need our Savior and His protection daily. We need to involve the Lord Jesus in our lives every day. Only *He* can deliver us and keep us safe!

Today's Prayer

*Father God, thank You that I never need to live in fear,
because my trust is in the Lord Jesus. I thank You that
though I am in this world, I am not of this world, and that
the enemy has no hold on me. I rejoice that I do not live
in fear because You will deliver me from the snare of the
fowler and from every perilous pestilence. Amen.*

Today's Thought

*Though I am in this world, I am not of this world.
My trust is in the Lord Jesus who delivers me from every
snare of the fowler and from every perilous pestilence.*

RIGHT PLACE, RIGHT TIME

*I returned and saw under the sun that—the race
is not to the swift, nor the battle to the strong, nor bread
to the wise, nor riches to men of understanding, nor favor
to men of skill;* **but time and chance happen to them
all***. For man also does not know his time: like fish
taken in a cruel net,* **like birds caught in a snare,**
*so the sons of men are snared in an evil time,
when it falls suddenly upon them.*

—*Ecclesiastes 9:11–12 (boldface mine)*

I want to share with you the Scripture above which, as in the previous reading, also talks about the fowler's snare. Sometimes, the best way to interpret Scripture is to ask the Holy Spirit for wisdom and revelation, look for recurring themes in the Bible, and allow Scripture to interpret Scripture. What I am saying is that there is a powerful truth here waiting to be unlocked, which we will see over the next six readings. Each reading builds upon the previous one, so I recommend going back to and refreshing your understanding of the previous teachings every day.

We have been reading Psalm 91:1 and Ecclesiastes 9:11. Did you notice that the number 911 occurs in both passages? The number 911 is very significant for our times. It is a number that marks the largest-scale terrorist attack on American soil to date. Our hearts were broken that day, the world changed, and we will never forget what happened. While I know that chapter and verse markers in our Bible aren't inspired, it is my personal opinion that the prayer of protection in Psalm 91 marks the times we are living in, and gives us a crystal clear reason why we *don't* have to live in fear.

In Ecclesiastes 9, King Solomon tells us that the winner of the race is not necessarily always the fastest one, and the person who wins the battle isn't necessarily always the strongest. He points out that men of understanding are not the only ones who gain riches, and men of skill do not always experience favor. And then he says this: "Time and chance happen to them all."

Solomon then goes on to talk about those who are "like fish taken in a cruel net" or "birds caught in a snare." (Notice that he's saying this of the "sons of men" and not the "sons of God." As believers, we are the sons and daughters of God.) There are therefore two categories of people—those who are blessed because they find themselves at the right place at the right time, and those who are caught off guard in an evil time and find themselves at the wrong place at the wrong time. I don't know about you, but I know which category I want to fall under!

As a son or daughter of God, rest assured that the blessing of being placed in the right place at the right time is yours because of our Lord Jesus! Despite the dangerous times we live in, you can expect Him to protect and deliver you from every snare of the enemy.

Today's Prayer

Heavenly Father, thank You that the race is not to the swift, nor the battle to the strong, nor favor to the skilled. You have made it possible for me to be at the right place at the right time. I declare that through Jesus' finished work, I am blessed to not be caught off guard in an evil time or find myself at the wrong place at the wrong time. Amen.

Today's Thought

As a child of the Most High God, I am blessed to be at the right place at the right time.

TIME AND CHANCE

*The race is not to the swift, nor the battle to the strong, nor bread to the wise, nor riches to men of understanding, nor favor to men of skill; but **time** and **chance happen** to them all.*

—*Ecclesiastes 9:11 (boldface mine)*

I want you to know how you can have "time and chance" happen to you like the first group of people I spoke about previously. Let me show you what the original Hebrew language reveals about how this can be your reality.

The Hebrew word for "time" is the word *eth*, meaning time or season.[7] The Hebrew words for "chance happen" are *pega qarah*. Together with *eth*, they present a picture not of random occurrences, but "right happenings" that are dependent on *the Lord's orchestration*. It's unfortunate that the word "chance" is used in the English translation. When you read "time and chance happen to them all," it gives the impression of random happenings, occurrences that happen as if by "luck."

But if you study the root of the word *pega* in the Scriptures, you'll see it is from the word *paga*, which actually means to make intercession or pray.[8] Let me introduce to you at this point a principle of Bible interpretation called the law of first mention. When you are studying a word, look at the first time it appears in the Bible. There is a lot of spiritual truth and significance in the first occurrence of the word in the Bible.

Applying this principle to the word *paga*, we see in the Bible that the first time it is used is in Genesis 23:8 (NIV), where it means "intercede." The same word is also used in Isaiah 53:12 where it says the Lord "**made intercession** for the transgressors" (boldface mine).

The other Hebrew word, *qarah*, is often used in other parts of the Bible to explain God-ordained happenings. So "chance happen" should more accurately be translated as "prayed opportunities" or "prayed happenings." When you have *eth* and *pega qarah* combined here, it speaks of *right-time, right-place happenings,* or *of being at the right place at the right time, doing the right thing as a result of prayer.* What an amazing blessing to possess, which is simply triggered by coming to our loving Father in heaven and expressing our dependence on His protection over us and our families. I want this blessing activated every day, don't you?

Today's Prayer

Father, thank You that my life is not subject to random occurrences that others often refer to as luck or fate. Thank You that as I look to You, depend on You, and live in the secret place of Your protection, You orchestrate the happenings in my life. I believe that the right-time, right-place happenings in my life come from Your divine orchestration and positioning. Amen.

Today's Thought

I believe I shall experience right-time, right-place happenings in my life as a result of prayer and dependence on my Lord Jesus.

THE HOLY SPIRIT LEADS US THROUGH PEACE

*Then the dove came to him **in the evening**, and behold,*
a freshly plucked olive leaf was in her mouth; and Noah
knew that the waters had receded from the earth.
—*Genesis 8:11 (boldface mine)*

Building upon the previous teaching, let's take a look at the first mention of *eth* (remember, it means "right timing") in the Bible. This word first appears in the phrase "in the evening" in the passage above. What do you see? The first mention of right timing has to do with the dove—that's a picture of the Holy Spirit. It's the Holy Spirit who can guide you to be at the right place at the right time.

But look at what the dove has in its mouth—an olive leaf. When the flood during Noah's time ended, God sent a message through the dove bearing a leaf that there would be no more such worldwide flooding and destruction (see Gen. 9:15). It was a message of peace to men. It tells us that the message the Holy Spirit brings is one of peace.

My friend, the Holy Spirit leads us on the wavelength of

peace. Sometimes, when you are about to do something, perhaps sign an agreement, plan a vacation, or take part in some activity, you might feel a lack of peace. If that happens, please stop and take time to pray about what you are about to do because the Holy Spirit speaks to us through the peace (or lack of it) He puts in us. He doesn't speak to us through nagging or accusations. He leads us through peace. When there is no peace in your heart, it's time for you to reevaluate your decision and listen to His leading.

There's another beautiful truth hidden in the first occurrence of the word *eth*. *Eth* appears in the phrase "in the evening" not only in Genesis 8:11, but in other parts of the Bible as well (see Gen. 24:11, Josh. 10:27). When I studied it, I realized that evening time is the time of our Lord Jesus' finished work at the cross.

The Old Testament priests had two daily sacrifices, one in the morning at 9 a.m. and the other in the evening at 3 p.m. Jesus was crucified at 9 a.m. and He died at 3 p.m., thus fulfilling the type of both the morning and evening sacrifices. At the time of the evening sacrifice, all of God's judgment had fallen on the body of Jesus. The floods of God's judgment were ended by the sacrifice of Christ. The Holy Spirit comes to you speaking peace, telling you that there is now no enmity between you and God, because judgment has passed. You are not perfect but you can have peace with God, and you can ask Him for success and be confident of His covering in all that you do because all your sins have been judged in the body of Christ!

Today's Prayer

*Lord Jesus, thank You for taking all of God's judgment
upon Yourself on the cross. Through Your perfect sacrifice,
I have peace with God. Thank You that the Holy Spirit has
come and will guide me with peace to be at the right
place at the right time. Help me to always hear
His voice and heed His leading. Amen.*

Today's Thought

*Because of Jesus' finished work on the cross, I have
peace with God and peace in my heart as I listen to
and follow the leading of the Holy Spirit.*

DAY 5

PRAY FOR RIGHT HAPPENINGS

The earnest prayer of a righteous person has great power and produces wonderful results.

—James 5:16 NLT

On Day 3 of this section, I showed you that the Hebrew word *qarah* is often used in the Bible to explain God-ordained happenings. The first time *qarah* is mentioned is in Genesis 24:12, when Abraham sent his servant to get a bride for his son, Isaac. The servant did not know which girl would be the right one, so he *prayed*, "O LORD God of my master Abraham, **please give me success** this day, and show kindness to my master Abraham" (boldface mine). The phrase "please give me success" is the word *qarah*. The servant asked God to give him *qarah*—right happening. Doesn't that remind you of what we said earlier about *pega qarah* being "prayed happenings"? If you follow the story, you will see how Abraham's servant was successful in his task.

What I want you to focus on here is the posture of the servant. He prayed for God's help, intervention, and leading.

He had a posture of humility. We all need the Lord in our daily lives. No matter how intelligent we are, we can't put ourselves at the right place at the right time a hundred percent of the time. Only the Lord can do this for us. If we stay "low" and lean on the Lord for wisdom, guidance, and understanding, He will guide us and protect us. To pray is to adopt a posture of humility. It is saying to God, "Father, I can't, but You can."

A lady who attends our church regularly shared that on one of her overseas trips, she got so engrossed in her quiet time with the Lord that she missed breakfast in the hotel at which she was staying. But while she was in her room, a horrific terror attack took place in the hotel's restaurant. She was dwelling in the secret place of the Most High and was supernaturally led to linger in His presence that morning. She humbly prioritized her time with the Lord over the scheduled time for her breakfast. If she had gone down to eat, she would have been at the wrong place at the wrong time.

That is why I like to call Psalm 91 the *prayer of protection*. When we pray this prayer, we are saying, "Lord Jesus, we can't protect ourselves, but You can. We humble ourselves before You. Be our refuge, our fortress, and our God. Surely You shall protect us and deliver us from harm in these dangerous times. Lead us to be at the right place at the right time and to be with the right people."

Today's Prayer

Father in heaven, I humble myself before You and readily agree that I need Your wisdom, guidance, and understanding. I can't always protect myself or my loved ones from harm in these dangerous times, but You can. I ask You to always lead us to be at the right place at the right time. I declare that You are my refuge, my fortress, and my God. Amen.

Today's Thought

I cannot always put myself at the right place at the right time, but God can. I humble myself before Him and lean on Him for wisdom and right timing in all that I do.

DAY 6

NOT BY ACCIDENT
OR COINCIDENCE

*And she **happened to come to** the part of*
the field belonging to Boaz.
                    —Ruth 2:3 (boldface mine)

⌇

In the previous reading, we looked at the first time the word *qarah* is used in the Bible. Another time *qarah* appears is in the above passage. I like how the King James Version puts it: "and her **hap was to light on** a part of the field *belonging unto Boaz*" (boldface mine). The Hebrew word for "to come to" and "to light on" here is *qarah*. And the Hebrew word for "happened" and "hap" here is *miqreh*, which comes from the word *qarah*.[9] Incidentally, the word *happy* comes from the old English word "hap," which is why when happenings happen the way you want them to happen, you are happy!

I don't know how many times I have heard testimonies from people who *happened* to meet an old friend in need and were able to minister to the friend, or who *happened* to have been delayed or who *happened* to change their original plans and, because of that, were protected from danger. My friend, none of those things happened by accident or coincidence. It was the Lord giving them *eth* and *qarah*—putting them at the right place at the right time!

This is reflected in a praise report from Sandy, who lives in Singapore.

Before I drive, I always make it a point to pray for protection. On March 31, I prayed as usual before I started driving toward the city.

I got stuck in heavy traffic and the cars were inching forward toward a major traffic junction. Like many motorists, I got impatient and was disappointed when the traffic light turned red just as I was approaching the junction. Then, I heard a strange sound of something cracking, and I was shocked as a huge old tree fell and hit the roof of the car right in front of me, creating a huge dent in its roof and shattering the rear windscreen.

By God's grace, the driver of the car emerged unscathed. Needless to say, I was very grateful to God when I realized that He had placed me at the right place at the right time so that I wasn't hurt.

I am very thankful to Jesus for His divine protection. Without His wings of protection over me, I may not even be alive today. Thank You, Jesus!

Even with something as mundane as driving on the road, which many of us do every day, we need to make it a point to pray for the Lord's protection. Let's not put our trust in our daily routines, our skills, or our limited ability to foresee danger. Our trust must be in the Lord's protection.

―――――

Today's Prayer

Abba, Father, help me to honor You and recognize Your hand at work whenever I experience deliverance from danger. As I go about the mundane routine activities of my life, I ask You for patience, wisdom, and guidance. I believe that You will always place me at the right place at the right time to protect me and keep me safe. Amen.

Today's Thought

The God of right-place, right-time happenings watches over my life. He gives me eth *and* qarah, *putting me at the right place at the right time to protect and bless me!*

DAY 7

JESUS HAS THE FINAL SAY

*"I am the Alpha and the Omega, the Beginning
and the End, the First and the Last."*

—*Revelation 22:13*

I want to show you one last thing about the phrase we have been studying, "but time and chance happen to them all" (Eccl. 9:11). Look at the phrase as written in Hebrew:

| to them all | *Tav Aleph* | happen | and chance | time | but |

Pay attention to the two Hebrew characters that I highlighted—*Aleph* and *Tav* (reading from right to left). *Aleph* and *Tav* are the first and last letters of the Hebrew alphabet. They are usually left untranslated in the Hebrew, and till today, most Jewish people do not know what the two letters combined really stand for. But in the New Testament book of Revelation, our Lord Jesus said, "I am the Alpha and the Omega" (see Rev. 1:8, 11). The New Testament is written in Greek, but Jesus being a Jew must have said, "I am the *Aleph* and the *Tav*."

He is the first letter and the last letter. The beginning and the end. So the letters *AlephTav* point to our Lord Jesus, who has the first and final word on your situations. Your diseases don't have the last word; He does. Your problems don't have the final say; He does.

His signature is inscribed in Ecclesiastes 9:11. Do you know what this means? It means that our Lord Jesus is the One who brings the *eth* and *qarah* together in your life! When your heart is full of and dependent on our Lord Jesus, you'll end up at the right place at the right time supernaturally!

As I mentioned in section 1, the prayer of protection is not an incantation or some magical chant that grants you protection. It is all about intimacy and relationship with the Lord. Prayer is a conversation. There is no relationship if there is no conversation. So talk to Him, commune with Him, involve Him, and listen to Him. He will lead and guide you to be at the right place at the right time with the right people.

The fowler's snare blends seamlessly into ordinary life for the unsuspecting bird—but so does the Lord's protection and intervention when you trust Him with your protection. It may play out so naturally you may not even realize you are being protected! As we heard from Sandy in the previous reading, even if you are stuck in a traffic jam, rejoice—it could be the Lord's way of positioning you and delivering you from some snare that you don't even know lies ahead! When you choose to involve the Lord and lean on His protection, you can live in rest and with confidence that He is watching over you.

Today's Prayer
*Beloved Lord Jesus, You are the Alpha and the Omega,
the Beginning and the End, the First and the Last.
Thank You that You have the first and final word on
anything that pertains to my life. I believe that You will
lead and guide me to be at the right place at the right time
with the right people. I thank You that right now,
You are working behind the scenes to deliver me
from every snare of the enemy. Amen.*

Today's Thought
Our Lord Jesus, the Aleph *and the* Tav, *has the first and
final word on my situations. Diseases do not have the final
word, nor do problems have the final say; He does!*

SECTION IV

CONSENT TO COME UNDER HIS WINGS

He shall cover you with His feathers,
And under His wings you shall take refuge;
His truth shall be your shield and buckler.

—*Psalm 91:4*

DAY 1

COME UNDER HIS WINGS OF MERCY AND GRACE

He shall cover you with His feathers, and under
His wings you shall take refuge.

—*Psalm 91:4*

❧

It is wonderful when the Lord delivers you from the snare of the fowler. But Psalm 91 tells us that God wants us to step into something even better. Verse 4 goes on to say, "He shall cover you with His feathers, and under His wings you shall take refuge." There are so many powerful truths hidden in this simple line!

The Old Testament was writ-ten predominantly to the Jewish people, who would understand words such as "His wings" and "feathers" as pointing to the ark of the covenant. Looking at the cherubim on top of the ark, you can see why.

The ark of the covenant.

Of all the furniture pieces in the temple, the ark was the

most holy. It was placed in the Holy of Holies, and typifies our Lord Jesus Christ. It was made of incorruptible wood and overlaid with gold. The wood represents His incorruptible and sinless humanity, while the gold speaks of His perfect divinity and deity. Our Lord Jesus was one hundred percent man and yet one hundred percent God. The lid of the ark of the covenant, where you find the cherubim, was hammered out of one solid piece of gold. It is called *kapporeth* in Hebrew and is usually translated as "mercy seat."[10] To understand the significance of the mercy seat, we have to understand the contents within the ark of the covenant.

Three items were placed inside the ark of the covenant: the stone tablets on which God had inscribed the Ten Commandments, a golden pot of manna, and Aaron's rod that had budded. The three items typify man's rebellion—man's rejection of God's holy standards, man's rejection of God's provision, and man's rejection of God's appointed leadership. God took these symbols of man's rebellion and failure, placed them in the ark of the covenant, and covered them with His mercy seat. It's a beautiful picture of His unmerited favor over our lives, of how mercy triumphs over judgment. This is the secret place where God wants you and me to live each day— not under the claws of judgment, punishment, and condemnation, but under His wings of mercy, grace, and favor. This is the place of intimacy with our Lord Jesus; this is the place of divine protection.

Today's Prayer
Lord Jesus, thank You for dying for my sins on the cross so that I can always receive Your goodness and protection in my life. Thank You that I can live each day under Your wings of mercy, grace, and favor, and not under the claws of judgment, punishment, and condemnation. I declare Your unmerited favor over my life. Amen.

Today's Thought
The secret place of divine protection where God wants me to live each day is under His wings of mercy, grace, and favor.

WHERE GOD MEETS AND SPEAKS WITH YOU

*"And there I will meet with you, and I will speak
with you from above the mercy seat."*

—Exodus 25:22

In Old Testament times, once a year, on Yom Kippur, or the Day of Atonement, the high priest would go into the Holy of Holies and sprinkle the blood of an innocent animal on the mercy seat. After the blood of the sacrifice was sprinkled on the mercy seat, all God saw of the ark of the covenant was the blood, and no longer the rebellion and failure of man as noted in the previous reading. However, under the old covenant, the blood of the animal sacrifices only *covered* the sins of the children of Israel for one year. What happened on Yom Kippur was only a *shadow*. Our Lord Jesus is the *substance*. He is the Lamb of God who *takes away* the sins of the world, and His sacrifice on the cross was once and for all (see John 1:29, Heb. 9:12)!

In Exodus 25:17–22, the Lord told Moses, "You shall make a mercy seat of pure gold....And you shall make two cherubim of gold; of hammered work you shall make them at the two ends of the mercy seat....*of one piece* with the mercy seat. And the cherubim shall stretch out *their* wings above, covering the mercy seat with their wings, and they shall face one another; the faces of the cherubim *shall be* toward the mercy seat. You shall put the mercy seat on top of the ark, and in the ark you shall put the Testimony that I will give you. And there I will meet with you, and I will speak with you from above the mercy seat, from between the two cherubim which *are* on the ark of the Testimony, about everything which I will give you in commandment to the children of Israel."

Where will the Lord speak from? From above the mercy seat. That is what my ministry is all about. I am preaching from above the mercy seat, preaching about His mercy and grace, about His shed blood, and about His finished work. There are people who are preaching from the judgment seat, preaching about the law and how we have fallen short. The wages of sin is death. Under the law, there is no escaping death. But this ministry is all about the Lord's mercy, grace, favor, love, and protection.

Under grace, Jesus died our death on the cross. He was punished with the death we deserved for our sins. He gave up His protection on the cross, so that we may walk in divine protection today. Hallelujah! Doesn't this just fill your heart with assurance and peace today?

Today's Prayer

Father God, thank You that the Lord Jesus is
Your Lamb who on the cross took away my sins once
and for all. Thank You for meeting with me and speaking
to me from above the mercy seat, and for reminding
me that I am in such a place of intimacy with You.
Because You love me, I believe that Your mercy, grace,
favor, love, and protection are mine. Amen.

Today's Thought

Jesus is the Lamb of God who was punished with the death
I deserved for my sins. He gave up His protection on the
cross so that I can walk in divine protection today.

NO SAFER PLACE IN THE UNIVERSE

*But Mary stood outside by the tomb weeping, and as she
wept she stooped down and looked into the tomb. And
she saw two angels in white sitting, one at the head and
the other at the feet, where the body of Jesus had lain.*

—John 20:11–12

❧

Do you know what Mary saw as she looked into the tomb?
She saw the *substance* of the ark of the covenant. Just as we
saw that there were two cherubim or angels on the mercy seat,
there were two angels sitting where Jesus had lain—one at the
head and the other at the feet. It was an empty tomb that our
Savior was laid in after He had paid the full price for our sins
with His own blood. Today, this tomb remains empty because
all our sins are forgiven and our Lord is risen! Our hope,
confidence, and assurance of salvation are found in the nail-
pierced hands of our resurrected Savior. The mercy seat is a
picture of the throne of grace (see Heb. 4:16). That is where
we want to be—at the throne of grace, under the protective
covering of His feathers and His wings.

I want to encourage you with this praise report from Veronica, who lives in New York City.

A few nights ago my husband, Casey, and I were stuck in a traffic jam for five hours. So we put on a sermon by Pastor Joseph Prince titled The Secret Place Where You Find Protection and Long Life. *Later, we found out that a fatal accident had taken place just five seconds ahead of us before we got stuck. Five seconds. The Lord had protected us from the accident!*

Today, Casey was again protected miraculously. It appeared that a driver had had a heart attack while driving and passed out. It led to a chain collision and all the cars in front of and behind Casey got hit. And the drivers were taken to the hospital.

Despite all this, Casey's car was completely untouched. Everything happened so quickly that he had no time to react. It was the Lord who protected him once again because that very morning, Casey was reading a devotional by Pastor Prince that drew Bible references from Psalm 91…."He shall cover you with His feathers, and under His wings you shall take refuge."

Truly, there is no safer place in the universe than under the protective shelter of our Savior's wings. What blessed assurance we can have today, knowing that even if destruction rages around us, there is always refuge and comfort in the Lord, our unfailing peace, protection, and supply.

I completely agree with Veronica that there is no safer place in the universe than under His wings, and I rejoice that the Lord's protection over her and Casey is for us as well!

Today's Prayer

Lord Jesus, thank You for being my Savior, and for paying the full price for my sins with Your blood. Thank You that Your resurrection is my hope, confidence, and assurance of salvation. I declare that there is no safer place for me than at the throne of grace, under the protective covering of Your feathers and wings. Amen.

Today's Thought

The safest place in the universe for me is under the protective covering of my Savior's wings.

GATHERED UNDER HIS WINGS

"O Jerusalem, Jerusalem, the one who kills the prophets and stones those who are sent to her! **How often I wanted to gather your children together, as a hen gathers her brood under her wings***, but you were not willing! See! Your house is left to you desolate."*

—*Luke 13:34–35 (boldface mine)*

There's another beautiful picture hidden in verse 4 of Psalm 91. It's a picture of a mother hen protecting her chicks. The Scriptures above record how the Lord Jesus looked at Jerusalem and lamented over it. Later, Jesus *wept* over Jerusalem, saying, "For days will come upon you when your enemies will build an embankment around you, surround you and close you in on every side, and level you, and your children within you, to the ground; and they will not leave in you one stone upon another, because you did not know the time of your visitation" (Luke 19:43–44). The Greek word for "wept" in verse 41 is *klaio*, and it means to be so affected emotionally as to sob and wail aloud.[11]

Can you see the Lord's tender mercies toward Israel as He shed much tears over her? He wished that He could gather Israel under His feathers as a mother hen gathers her chicks under her wings, but the Lord could not force His protection on them because they rejected Him. I believe that as our Lord wept, He foresaw not only the Roman siege of Jerusalem, when the temple was burned to the ground and many of the Jews killed or sold as slaves, but He also foresaw the horrors of the Holocaust.

Notice that the Lord said, "But you were not willing!" This clearly tells us that the Lord will not force on us His protection if we are not willing to come under His wings. Beloved, are you willing to have the Lord Jesus protect you and your family today? Then tell Him. Let's never take our Lord's protection for granted. Instead, let's take time daily to let Him know that we are putting our trust in Him for His covering and protection.

Do you want to know what happens when you do that? Look at what Boaz said to Ruth: "The LORD repay your work, and a full reward be given you by the LORD God of Israel, under whose wings you have come for refuge" (Ruth 2:12). Wow! It was already a privilege for this Moabite outcast, who was disqualified by the law, to find refuge under the wings of the God of Israel. But God even rewarded her for doing so. In the same way, it is a privilege for us to be able to take refuge under His wings. Yet when we tell the Lord that we need Him and want His refuge, He gives us a full reward for trusting Him and for coming under His wings. What a God!

Today's Prayer

Lord Jesus, thank You for Your tender mercies over me, that You would gather me under Your wings as a mother hen gathers her chicks under her wings. I welcome Your protection today over me and my family. I declare that I am putting my trust in You for Your covering and protection over us everywhere we go and in everything we do. Amen.

Today's Thought

Today and every day, I need the Lord Jesus and I put my trust in Him for His covering and protection.

INTIMACY WITH THE LORD

*"Come to Me, all you who labor and are heavy laden,
and I will give you rest. Take My yoke upon you and
learn from Me, for I am gentle and lowly in heart,
and you will find rest for your souls."*

—*Matthew 11:28–29*

The Lord does not want you to simply claim His promises of protection. He wants you to come close to Him. Running to Him and coming under His feathers speak of closeness. It's not about how many times you have recited Psalm 91; it's about having an intimate relationship with Him. As a child, if it was thundering at night and I was afraid, I would run into my parents' room, jump into their bed, and hide in my mother's arms. After a while, I would fall into a deep sleep even if the storm was still raging outside. You see, you don't have to learn the seven steps of overcoming fear. Having the presence of a loving parent right with you is enough to drive out fear. Our Lord Jesus who loves you wants you to come close to Him and to take shelter in His love. Will you do that today?

I heard the story of a farmer whose farmhouse got burned down. As he walked around the smoldering wreckage, he saw the burned carcasses of his chickens. He happened to move the blackened body of one of the hens with his foot, and to his astonishment, little chicks came running out from under the body. What happened? They had taken refuge under the wings of their mother, who had given her life to save her little ones.

That's a picture of what our Lord Jesus did when He took upon His own body the full punishment for our sins. The fire of God's judgment fell, not upon the scribes and Pharisees who had rejected the Messiah, and not upon the Roman soldiers who nailed Him to the cross, but upon His own beloved Son—for the nation of Israel, for the Gentile nations, for you, for me, so that whosoever believes in Him would be saved.

But here's something I want you to see: when Jesus was offered on the cross, He absorbed the judgment of God in His own body, and, as the sacrifice, He was greater than the fires of judgment. The Offering was greater than the judgment because the Offering was not consumed. On that cross, our Lord declared, "It is finished!" *before* He gave up His Spirit (John 19:30). The Offering remained *after* all of God's judgment was exhausted. Hallelujah! That is why we can come boldly to His throne of grace today!

Today's Prayer
*Abba, Father, thank You that You want me to come close
to You because You love me. Thank You that my Lord Jesus
took the full punishment for my sins and that I can now
come boldly to Your throne of grace to receive all the
help and protection I need. I take shelter in Your
love that drives out all my fears. Amen.*

Today's Thought
*The Lord Jesus loves me and wants me to be close to Him
and to take shelter in His love and presence.*

COME BOLDLY

Let us therefore come boldly to the throne of grace, that we may obtain mercy and find grace to help in time of need.

—Hebrews 4:16

Beloved, when we are willing to have the Lord Jesus protect us and our family, and we take time daily to let Him know we are putting our trust in Him, we receive His abundant mercies for needs that transcend our understanding. I received a praise report from Victoria who lives in California that vividly illustrates how the Lord protects us when we simply come boldly to His throne of grace and humbly consent to be protected by Him. This is what Victoria shared with me:

> Sometime ago, I was replaying your on-demand Web broadcast. At the end of the message, you said you would pray for our protection. I quickly put the message on pause and called my seventeen-year-old daughter to come and receive the prayer and blessing with me.
>
> During the prayer, you prayed that we would not die in our sleep. Though we did not have that fear, we received the prayer gladly anyway.

The next morning, when I woke up, I felt really ill, to the point I didn't think I could go to work. When I went to wake my daughter to go to school, she was also unwell, complaining of the same symptoms I was experiencing. Sensing something amiss, we both went to the ER and found out we had carbon monoxide poisoning from a faulty heater!

We know and have heard reports of how people who were exposed to carbon monoxide while asleep usually died in their sleep. We believe we were saved because of the prayer you prayed over us and our receiving it. God heard and answered. He woke us up just in time so we could be saved. We give Jesus all the glory!

What a powerful testimony of a believer who takes every opportunity to come to the throne of grace and gladly consent to come under the Lord's wings of protection! I pray you'll be encouraged to do the same every day.

Today's Prayer
Father in heaven, thank You that I can simply come
boldly to Your throne of grace and consent to be protected
by You. I believe that as I put my trust in You, I will receive
Your abundant mercies and find the grace to help
in time of any need I may have. Amen.

Today's Thought
I come boldly to God's throne of grace today and take
shelter in His presence and love.

SHIELDED FROM EVERY DEVICE OF THE ENEMY

His truth shall be your *shield and buckler.*

—*Psalm 91:4*

Psalm 91:4 starts with "He shall cover you with His feathers, and under His wings you shall take refuge" and ends with this proclamation: "His truth *shall be your* shield and buckler." What is the shield and buckler? A buckler refers to a small round shield used for close-contact fighting. A shield is much larger, one you can dig into the ground and hide behind when spears, arrows, or rocks are being launched at you in a bigger attack. So whether it is a small or big attack, His truth—your shield and buckler—covers you completely!

In Ephesians 6:16, it tells us to, *above all*, take the shield of faith to quench *all* the fiery darts of the wicked one. Why? Because the shield of faith will cover you all around. Amen! That is why the devil is after your shield of faith—he wants to make you doubt God's Word, which is His truth. Once you take up the shield of faith, his attacks against you cannot prosper. So lift up your shield!

My dear reader, as you listen to messages about Jesus' finished work and your faith is being built, your shield is also being built. Even if you are found in the wrong place at the wrong time, the Lord can protect you when His shield of faith surrounds you and you are placed under the shadow of His wings.

One of our church members was driving on the freeway with his family and came behind a van that had a queen-size mattress tied to its roof. Suddenly, the ropes that secured the mattress to the van snapped and the mattress came hurtling toward his vehicle. He and his wife braced themselves for impact, expecting the large mattress to crash into their windscreen, since there was no way they could avoid it in time.

Miraculously, the mattress somehow hit the road just in front of their car, bounced to the side, and hit another car instead. Thankfully, the driver of that car was able to brake in time and did not cause an accident. For our church member, it was as if a force field—or an invisible shield—had protected his whole family! Can you imagine what could have happened if that large mattress had crashed into the windscreen of his car, which was ferrying his wife as well as their young children in the backseat? Let's give thanks to the Lord, for He is so good and His tender mercies endure forever! Truly, *He shall cover you with His feathers, and under His wings you shall take refuge.*

Today's Prayer
Father God, I give You thanks that Your truth is my shield and buckler and covers me completely in every battle, whether the attack is small or big. Thank You for Your Word that shows me how You are willing and able to deliver and protect me no matter what dangers surround me. I declare that no attack against me will prosper. Amen.

Today's Thought
I am covered completely by Your Word and Your promises which are my shield of faith that quenches all the fiery darts of the wicked one.

SECTION V

FEARLESS LIVING

You shall not be afraid of the terror by night,
Nor of the arrow that flies by day,
Nor of the pestilence that walks in darkness,
Nor of the destruction that lays waste at noonday.

—*Psalm 91:5–6*

DAY 1

HOW TO LIVE FEARLESSLY

You shall not be afraid of the terror by night,
nor *of the arrow* that *flies by day,* nor *of the pestilence*
that *walks in darkness,* nor *of the destruction*
that *lays waste at noonday.*

—*Psalm 91:5–6*

I love how Psalm 91 reminds us that we have round-the-clock protection. Whether it is at night or in the day. Whether it is in darkness or at noonday. Whether we are faced with a terror or confronted by arrows. Whether pestilences threaten or destruction looms. We do *not* have to be afraid because our God, who watches over us, neither slumbers nor sleeps (see Ps. 121:3–4)!

The reality is, the world we live in seems to be engulfed in negative news and fear. We often hear reports of senseless terrorist attacks on innocent civilians, horrific accidents claiming multiple victims, or an epidemic affecting entire communities, leading to hundreds of babies being born with deformities. I know that many can't help but dread that the same tragedies could befall them.

But beloved, I want you to know that in the midst of all that is happening in the world, you *can* be fearless, and this comes from knowing the Lord as the God of peace.

Romans chapter 15 ends with the apostle Paul saying, "Now the **God of peace** *be* with you all" (Rom. 15:33, boldface mine). You might ask, *Isn't God with us all the time? Why then did Paul specifically say, "The God of peace be with you all"?* What Paul was speaking over the people was for God to manifest Himself as the God of peace in their lives. In other words, even though God is always with us, we may not always experience Him as the God of peace.

Do you know what happens when God manifests Himself as the God of peace in your life? Romans 16:20 (boldface mine) tells us this: "And the **God of peace will crush Satan** under your feet shortly. The **grace** of our Lord Jesus Christ *be* with you. Amen."

Do you see what the God of peace will do in your life? He will crush every fear, every worry, and every anxiety!

Do you see *grace* in that verse as well? Grace—the undeserved, unearned, and unmerited favor of God—is the only thing against which the devil has no defense. That is why we put our faith in the blood of Jesus when we talk about protection. His sinless blood was shed to pay the price for the guilty one. And because Jesus paid the price, we who are in Him have a right to walk in divine health and protection. Grace qualifies us for God's all-encompassing protection. Amen!

Today's Prayer
Lord Jesus, I ask You to manifest as the God of peace in my life today. I thank You that there is nothing that I need to fear because You watch over me night and day. Thank You for being with me and crushing Satan under my feet. I declare that because of Your grace, I have victory over every fear, every worry, and every anxiety. Amen.

Today's Thought
The God of peace is with me and crushes Satan along with every fear, every worry, and every anxiety through His grace.

DAY 2

THE POWER OF HIS LOVE AND GRACE

*And the God of peace will crush Satan under
your feet shortly. The grace of our Lord Jesus
Christ be with you. Amen.*

—*Romans 16:20*

In the previous reading, we saw that grace is the only thing against which the devil has no defense. If you are living by your self-effort to earn God's approval, the devil has power over you because he can always point to something that you have not done. This gives him dominion over you. If you claim God's protection and healing based on what you have done, the devil, who is a master accuser, just has to point to one of your failures, and all your faith implodes. You will disqualify yourself mentally and inwardly from receiving whatever you might be trusting the Lord for.

But grace qualifies us for protection. Because Jesus paid the price, we who are in Him have a right to walk in divine health and protection. When the devil accuses you, saying, "How dare you believe God for protection, when you are (he goes on to list your failures)," you just have to point to Jesus' blood, which has paid for all your failures. With grace as your basis, the God of peace can reign over your fears and impart to you unshakable faith for His protection!

Something else happens when you understand His grace—you will also grow in your understanding of how perfectly loved you are by your Father in heaven. God *so* loved you and me, He sent His only begotten Son to die on the cross on our behalf, carrying all our sins upon His own body so that today, we can come boldly to His throne of grace. He did it so that today, we are not as sheep without a shepherd, but we are so deeply loved and cared for by our Abba Father. We are His children and when we call on Him, He WILL answer. We have a God who demonstrated His love for us *while* we were still sinners—when we had nothing to offer Him but our brokenness, our shame, our sins, and our disqualifications! Oh what perfect love!

The Word of God says, "There is **no fear** in love; but **perfect love casts out fear**, because fear involves torment. But he who fears has not been made perfect in love. We love Him because He first loved us" (1 John 4:18–19, boldface mine). Are you fearful today? Ask yourself this question: Do you know how much God loves you? You see, you can't reason away fear. But when you have a revelation of His perfect love for you, every fear in your life will be cast out. To the extent that you understand His love for you, you will live fearlessly in dangerous times!

Today's Prayer
Abba, Father, thank You that the grace of my Lord Jesus qualifies me for the right to walk in health and protection. Thank You for Your perfect love that truly casts out every fear and enables me to live fearlessly. I declare that Jesus' blood has paid for all my failures and is my unshakable basis for Your protection. Amen.

Today's Thought
It is the grace of God that qualifies me for protection, not anything I have done or will do. It is the perfect love of God that casts out every fear from my life and enables me to live fearlessly.

JEHOVAH SHALOM
IS YOUR GOD

Now the God of peace be with you all. Amen.

—Romans 15:33

❦

I'm sure you want the Lord to manifest Himself as the God of peace when you are fearful. So let's go deeper into what the "God of peace" means. Don't forget that Paul was Jewish, so when he said "the God of peace *be* with you," he was saying "*Jehovah Shalom* be with you." "*Jehovah Shalom*" is Hebrew for "the God of peace." Now, the first appearance of the name *Jehovah Shalom* is in the Old Testament story of Gideon in Judges 6.

As we read Gideon's story, we discover that the Midianites terrorized Israel day and night, descending upon them like a swarm of marauding locusts and destroying their crops and pillaging their livestock. Fearful of their cruel enemies, the Israelites hid in dens and caves in the mountains. It is no wonder Gideon was petrified and hid himself at the bottom of an abandoned winepress to thresh the measly stalks of dry grain he had somehow managed to scavenge. He was bound by fear and overcome by all the news of terror that surrounded him.

In the midst of Gideon's fear, "the Angel of the LORD appeared to him, and said to him, 'The LORD *is* with you, you mighty man of valor!'" (Judg. 6:12).

When you find the expression "the Angel of the LORD" in the Old Testament, it usually refers to our Lord Jesus in His preincarnate state. Jesus Himself appeared to Gideon when he was in the pit of fear and called him a mighty man of valor. Isn't that amazing?

Are there moments when you feel besieged by fear? When you hear reports of terror or exposure to some virus, do you feel fearful and anxious? Has fear driven you into hiding? The truth is, regardless of how you feel, when our Lord Jesus looks at you right now, He sees you as a *mighty man or mighty woman of courage.*

Isn't it amazing how our Lord looks at us? It's not how we see ourselves that defines us; it is how our Lord Jesus sees us that defines us. That's why we read His Word. We read it to discover what His Word says about us. My friend, no matter what state you are in right now and how messed up your life might be, the Lord Jesus sees the best in you.

He sees your potential, your gifting, your call, and your destiny to do great things in this life! And as the ending of

Gideon's story shows, He will guide you and cause you to be a testimony of His protection as you trust in Him and see yourself and your situations through His eyes.

Today's Prayer

Jehovah Shalom, *my God of peace, thank You that no matter how I feel about myself, You see and call me a person of valor. Thank You that no matter how I see myself, You see me as a person of courage, and You are with me to lead, deliver, and provide me with a testimony of Your protection. I declare that Your Word, and Your Word alone, defines me. Amen.*

Today's Thought

No matter how I feel, my Jehovah Shalom, *the God of peace, sees me as a mighty person of courage. What He says in His Word about me defines my identity.*

HOW TO BE LED
BY HIS PEACE

Now may the Lord of peace Himself give you peace
always in every way. The Lord be with you all.
—2 Thessalonians 3:16

Let's continue Gideon's story from the previous reading. I want you to know that when God becomes *Jehovah Shalom*, the God of peace, in your life, He doesn't just soothe your emotions. He will *lead you with His peace*. For example, you may be making some decisions at your work, for your children, or perhaps even where and when to travel for your vacation. Talk to Jesus about it. He will lead and guide you with His peace. If there is peace from the Lord, go with that decision. If there is an absence of peace and you feel a sense of restraint, back away from it. You will find that guidance from the Lord comes very easily when God manifests Himself as *Jehovah Shalom*. In His peace, decisions don't feel forced and full of strife. In His peace, there is a rest. His peace will guide you supernaturally to be at the right place, at the right time, with the right people.

After our Lord called Gideon a man of valor, his response

was: "O my lord, if the LORD is with us, why then has all this happened to us? And where *are* all His miracles which our fathers told us about, saying, 'Did not the LORD bring us up from Egypt?' But now the LORD has forsaken us and delivered us into the hands of the Midianites" (Judg. 6:13).

Doesn't Gideon remind us of ourselves? Instead of hearing what the Lord had just called him, he began to complain. "Why has the Lord forsaken us?" Astoundingly, the Lord simply turned to him and said, "Go in this might of yours, and you shall save Israel from the hand of the Midianites. Have I not sent you?" (Judg. 6:14).

What? First, the Lord Jesus calls this man who is in hiding "a man of valor." Now, He calls this complaining man, who is mad at God, to go in that might of his and save Israel? Shouldn't it be, "Be gone from My presence, you stinking complainer, I must have found the wrong guy"?

I am so glad that the Lord is not like you and me. He always calls the things that are not as though they are (see Rom. 4:17). And I believe that as you receive a revelation of how the Lord is the God of peace in your life, you may be fearful and complaining now, but like Gideon, God will send you to be a testimony of His protection. He will send you to all your friends, coworkers, and loved ones who are bound by fear, and He will use you to deliver them from fear!

Today's Prayer

*Lord Jesus, thank You that I have Your promise
that You will lead and guide me with Your peace.
Thank You that as I am led by Your peace and rest,
You will guide me to be at the right place at the right
time with the right people. I believe that through Your
protection over my life, others will see Your goodness
and be delivered from fear. Amen.*

Today's Thought

*My Lord Jesus, the God of peace, will lead and guide
me with His peace to be at the right place at the
right time with the right people.*

JESUS GIVES YOU PEACE IN EVERY AREA

Then the LORD said to him, "Peace be with you; do not
fear, you shall not die." So Gideon built an altar there to
the LORD, and called it The-LORD-Is-Peace.

—Judges 6:23–24

There's still more to Gideon's story that I want to reveal to you. The account in Judges 6 tells us that even after Gideon had God's promise to "go in this might of yours" and save Israel, he was still fearful and unconvinced. He then asked for a sign to confirm that he was indeed speaking to the Lord. Gideon then presented an offering to the Lord, and fire rose out of the rock to consume the offering. Then our Lord Jesus disappeared. Only at that moment did Gideon's lightning-fast mind perceive that he had indeed been speaking with the Lord Himself. He gasped, "Alas, O Lord God! For I have seen the Angel of the LORD face to face" (Judg. 6:22).

Gideon began to panic, because in those days, they believed that if they saw God face to face, they would die. But before Gideon could frighten himself any further, the Lord said to him, "**Peace** *be* with you; **do not fear**, you shall not die" (Judg. 6:23, boldface mine). So Gideon built an altar there to the Lord and called it "The-Lord-*Is*-Peace" (Judg. 6:24), or in Hebrew, *Jehovah Shalom.* This is the first time the name *Jehovah Shalom* appears in the Bible, and the word that goes with this name is "you shall not die."

According to the *Strong's Concordance*, the word *shalom* refers to completeness, safety, soundness, welfare, health, and supply. It also refers to peace, quiet, tranquility, and contentment, as well as friendship in human relationships and with God in a covenant relationship.[12] So if you think that *Jehovah Shalom* just gives you peace of mind, you are wrong. When you receive the Lord as *Jehovah Shalom* in your life, you are receiving so much more!

My dear friends, I believe with all my heart that the Lord wants to speak to you today about the world we live in. Like Gideon, we may be surrounded by bad news, like news of diseases such as Ebola and Zika, of bomb attacks, of random shootings, of hijackings, of missile strikes, and of fatal accidents. But God has already foreseen the problems that we will face in this day and age, and His protection and covering over us is all-encompassing!

Today's Prayer

Lord Jesus, thank You that You command Your peace to be with me and for me to not be afraid. Thank You that Your peace covers all of my life—my welfare, health, mind, career, and relationships. I believe that You have already foreseen the problems I will face and that Your protection and covering is all-encompassing. Amen.

Today's Thought

God has already foreseen any problem I will face today. He is my peace and protection in the midst of every adversity.

YOU SHALL NOT
BE AFRAID

"Fear not, for I am with you; be not dismayed, for I am
your God. I will strengthen you, yes, I will help you,
I will uphold you with My righteous right hand."

—Isaiah 41:10

When Psalm 91 says you shall not be afraid of "the pestilence *that* walks in darkness," it speaks of every epidemic, every virus, every deadly disease, and every outbreak. When it mentions "the destruction *that* lays waste at noonday," it covers all accidents and outward destruction. When it talks about the "arrow *that* flies by night," it covers all projectiles, including even modern missiles that can shoot down planes.

Do you know what it means for something to "walk in darkness"? Doctors might tell you that they do not know what disease is developing in your body. Now, as a child of God, you can claim His promise straightaway and say, "I will *not* be afraid of the disease that walks in darkness." Do the necessary medical checks and consult with medical professionals, but do it without fear. Do it with your *Jehovah Shalom*. When you take God as your *Jehovah Shalom*, this is what He says to you: "Do not fear, you shall not die."

Some years ago, there was an outbreak of severe acute respiratory syndrome (SARS) in my nation of Singapore. A young woman was infected while abroad and triggered a series of transmissions after she returned to Singapore. The deadly SARS virus infected 238 other people. Sadly, 33 of them died. Outside of Singapore, more than 20 other countries reported infections by the virus. It was a global epidemic.

A heavy cloud of fear hung over the entire nation during this time. Every day, news outlets reported new infections and fatalities. It seemed like the spread of the virus was unstoppable. Most pointedly, a report indicated that "The most immediate impact of the new disease was fear. People stayed home more and avoided public or crowded places like swimming pools and shopping centers. Many also curbed their wanderlust and shelved travel plans."[13] But as a local church we continued to hold our services, which drew a regular attendance of over 8,000 people at that time.

During this period, I preached strongly on the prayer of protection in Psalm 91, and the church even gave out little cards with Psalm 91 printed on them to encourage our congregation to pray this prayer every day. I preached by faith on *Jehovah Shalom* and declared that as a church, the Lord's word for us in the midst of the SARS epidemic was what He told Gideon: "Do not fear, you shall not die." By God's amazing grace, *not one person* who was attending our church regularly died from this deadly virus. Hallelujah!

Today's Prayer

Father in heaven, thank You that there is nothing that I will ever face that is outside the bounds of Your amazing grace and protection. Based on the authority of Your Word, I declare that nothing that walks in darkness will prevail against me and that I shall not be afraid. Amen.

Today's Thought

Wherever I go and whatever I face, I take Jesus as my Jehovah Shalom and walk without fear.

NOTHING IS TOO HARD FOR THE LORD

"Behold, I am the LORD, the God of all flesh.
Is there anything too hard for Me?"

—Jeremiah 32:27

✧

Here is another praise report that I want to share with you. Tracy, who lives in Alaska, shared this powerful testimony of how the Lord delivered her brother from a serious disease that almost took his life:

A few months ago, my brother, Shane, contracted Guillain-Barré syndrome (a serious autoimmune disorder in which the body's immune system attacks the nervous system) in Laos. He was refused treatment by several hospitals in Laos and Thailand. They said he was far too advanced in the disease and that there was nothing they could do for him. He was finally able to receive treatment in a government hospital in Udon Thani, Thailand. But while there, he developed further complications and contracted three strains of pneumonia and methicillin-resistant Staphylococcus aureus (MRSA).

I flew all the way from the United States to Udon Thani and when I saw Shane, he looked like a man hours from death, almost completely paralyzed and hooked only to a ventilator. He could only move his lips and head a bit.

I quickly pronounced God's protection and provision, and called upon the grace and mercy of God to deliver us. Within twenty-eight hours of my arrival, Shane was transported via aircraft to a private hospital in Bangkok, Thailand. He was admitted directly to the intensive care unit (ICU) where, after the first day, he was able to move his arms.

His condition improved so quickly that all the doctors and hospital staff were in shock and awe. I told them that the miracle was from God. Even my sister-in-law, who was a non-believer, saw what God was doing and wanted to know this Jesus. In fact, she gave her heart to the Lord in the hospital! She had learned so much about the love of God during that time that even her family members began asking, "Who is this Jesus?"

On the sixth day after his admission, Shane was moved from the ICU to a private room and his condition continued to improve. It wasn't easy as he had severe pain and sleepless nights, but God was there every step of the way. Throughout the day, I would lay hands on him and pray over his body. Folks back home in the United States were also praying continually.

This was war—a battle like I'd never imagined. I rarely left the hospital room and I prayed continually. Every morning, Shane and I would talk about the Lord and what He was teaching us. I also read Shane bits of Joseph Prince's book, Unmerited Favor, *and encouraged myself in the Lord through the Word and through Joseph's book.*

Joseph's book was a source of strength. Prior to Shane's illness, I had been devouring Joseph's daily broadcasts and literature. I learned so much during that season and it prepared me for this battle. Through the healing process of my brother, I learned to lean on God and to know that He is good and always delivers. Healing is always available to us—sometimes instant, sometimes a process, but always available through the broken body and blood of Jesus.

Even though the typical recuperation time for this syndrome is between six months and three years, Shane was already walking one month later. Four months after, he was able to drive and to lift nearly 300 pounds of weight. Six months later, he went back to work full-time and was also completely delivered from depression, something he had been dealing with for a long time.

> *Thank you for staying true to the message of grace. It's all about Jesus and His COMPLETED work on the cross. Hallelujah!*

Praise the Lord! Truly, we do not have to be afraid of diseases that even doctors do not know how to deal with, or as Psalm 91 describes, "the pestilence *that* walks in darkness." The disease was "too advanced" for Shane's doctors, but it was not too advanced for the Lord who delivered him! He will do the same for you.

———

Today's Prayer

Father, there is no other God like You. Nothing is too hard for You and no disease or condition is too advanced for Your deliverance. Thank You for the broken body and blood of Jesus that completely heals and delivers me. I believe that You are with me every step of the way through every season of my life. Amen.

Today's Thought

Because of Jesus and His finished work on the cross, there is nothing that is too hard or too advanced for the Lord to deliver me from.

HIS PEACE WILL GUARD YOUR HEART AND MIND

*Be anxious for nothing, but in everything by prayer
and supplication, with thanksgiving, let your requests
be made known to God; and the peace of God,
which surpasses all understanding, will guard your
hearts and minds through Christ Jesus.*

—*Philippians 4:6–7*

Beloved, in the natural, there are so many reasons for us to be afraid. We can be fearful of terrorist attacks. We can be worried about contracting diseases and plagues. We can be anxious about destruction and accidents. Round the clock, there seems to be legitimate reasons for us to be filled with dread.

But there is a realm that is higher than what we see in the natural, and I declare to you today that YOU SHALL NOT BE AFRAID. Fear is a spiritual condition, and cannot be combated with a natural answer, or by us trying to reason it away. The Bible tells us that the natural mind cannot understand things that are spiritual (see 1 Cor. 2:14).

So how can you not be afraid? Invite the God of peace

to reign in your life. As you do that, the robust peace of God, which surpasses all understanding, *will* guard your heart and mind through Christ Jesus.

Beloved, as you allow the Lord Jesus to be your refuge and your hiding place, you can receive the peace that He gives. Today, hear your Lord Jesus whispering to you, "Peace I leave with you, My peace I give to you; not as the world gives do I give to you. Let not your heart be troubled, neither let it be afraid" (John 14:27). Receive His supernatural peace, which is beyond what is logical, beyond what your limited mind can comprehend. Receive His supernatural peace that will guard your heart and become a bulwark for your mind. And may *Jehovah Shalom,* our God of Peace, fill your heart and set you free to live fearlessly in these dangerous times!

Today's Prayer

Lord Jesus, thank You for giving me Your peace that surpasses understanding to guard my heart and mind. I invite You to reign in my life and be my refuge and hiding place. I believe that You are setting me free to live fearlessly in these dangerous times. Amen.

Today's Thought

I receive the peace that Jesus gives to me to guard my heart and mind. I will not be afraid because He is my refuge and fortress no matter where I am.

SECTION VI

IT SHALL NOT COME NEAR YOU

A thousand may fall at your side,
And ten thousand at your right hand;
But it shall not come near you.
Only with your eyes shall you look,
And see the reward of the wicked.

—Psalm 91:7–8

THE BATTLE IS REAL

A thousand may fall at your side, and ten thousand
at your right hand; but it shall not come near you.
Only with your eyes shall you look, and see
the reward of the wicked.

—*Psalm 91:7–8*

Imagine you are in a battlefield and all around you soldiers are being slain. On one side, you see a thousand fall. On the other, ten thousand crumple one by one to the ground. You hear screams as bullets find their targets.

It is a disturbing picture and I thank God that the majority of us have not had to experience the horrors of being in a physical combat zone. But that does not mean that we are not under attack nor does it mean that we do not see death claiming its victims all around us.

We are assaulted daily from all directions by tragic newsflashes, by doctors' reports, and by attacks of the devil launched at us. And every day, we see casualties around us as we read about people dying in accidents, in attacks, or of diseases. Please understand that I am not in any way suggesting that such occurrences are equivalent to the experiences of those who may have been in wars. What I do want to establish is that believers are in a spiritual war, and we should not be ignorant of the enemy's tactics.

When the enemy attacks you, do you recognize his weapons? The projectiles he shoots may not come with arrowheads or be filled with gunpowder, but they are no less deadly. His weapons come in the form of crippling thoughts and crushing fears. When you hear about a plane crash and are paralyzed by the thought that your next plane ride might be your last, you have been shot. When you read about a shooting at a concert venue and fear going near one in case the same thing happens to you, a "bullet" has been lodged in your mind.

In this section, I want to teach and equip you to combat these oppressive thoughts. Unfortunately, many believers who may experience these dark thoughts allow them to take root and grow. They water them with worry, fertilize them with anxiety, and allow them to sun for hours in their mind. How? By replaying the bad thoughts over and over again and letting them go on and on like a broken record. As a result, these believers can't sleep, they suffer from chronic panic attacks, and they might even develop autoimmune and psychosomatic conditions. What begins in the mind can take root in your heart, and can even lead to adverse effects on your physical body. When those negative thoughts come your way, you must *not* give them time to take root!

Today's Prayer

Father God, thank You for revealing to me that I am in a spiritual battle with an enemy I cannot see but who attacks with crippling thoughts and crushing fears. Thank You for Your Word that teaches and equips me to combat these oppressive thoughts. Help me to focus on Your love and Your promises for me so that these dark, negative thoughts do not take root in my heart. Amen.

Today's Thought

I chose to be rooted in God's love and protection promises for me, rather than allow the oppressive thoughts of the enemy to take root in my heart.

DAY 2

IT IS WRITTEN

Then Jesus said to him, "Away with you, Satan!
For it is written, 'You shall worship the LORD your God,
and Him only you shall serve.'"

—*Matthew 4:10*

I ended the previous reading by saying that when negative thoughts come your way, you must *not* give them time to take root in your heart. That correlates with the wise saying that you can't stop birds from flying over your head, but you can surely stop them from building a nest on your head. We can't stop the enemy from attacking our minds, but we can surely defend ourselves with the sword of the Spirit, which is the Word of God (see Eph. 6:17). God's Word is infallible, unshakable, and everlasting (see Isa. 40:8, 1 Pet. 1:25). Our Lord Jesus Himself showed us what to do when we are under attack by the devil. Three times He was tempted by Satan in the wilderness. Each time, His response was the same—He quoted the *written* Word of God. Against each attack, His response was to say, "It is written" (see Matt. 4:1–11).

I know of believers who say, "God spoke to me and told

me that He will do that for me." I want to encourage you not to go by what you think the Lord said to you. You cannot fight the devil by saying, "God spoke to me," apart from the written Word. Please understand that I am not at all against God speaking to you, but coming against the enemy and his attacks with "God spoke to me" is not what our Lord Jesus did.

My friend, if you want to combat the enemy's attacks, stick to the pattern that our Lord Jesus showed us. In the first temptation, the devil challenged our Lord Jesus to prove His identity, saying, "If You are the Son of God, command that these stones become bread" (Matt. 4:3). Don't you think it is interesting that our Lord did not rely on what His Father had audibly spoken over Him at the River Jordan? A voice had come from heaven, saying, "This is My beloved Son, in whom I am well pleased" (Matt. 3:17). Yet, the Lord did not point Satan to the spoken word of God. Over and over again, He declared, "It is written." Now, if the Son of God used "it is written" to defeat the devil, how much more you and I need to.

When fear grips your heart or evil thoughts plague your mind, *quote His written Word*!

Today's Prayer

*Lord Jesus, thank You for showing me what to do
when I am under attack by the devil. Thank You
for giving me the sword of the Spirit, Your infallible,
unshakable, and everlasting Word, to defeat every
fear and every evil thought. I believe that
Your Word is my sure defense. Amen.*

Today's Thought

*When the enemy attacks my mind with fear and
evil thoughts, I have God's infallible, unshakable, and
everlasting Word to declare by faith over my situation.*

APPLYING THE WRITTEN WORD

But the righteousness of faith speaks....But what does it
say? "The word is near you, in your mouth and in your
heart" (that is, the word of faith which we preach).

—Romans 10:6, 8

꧁

Let me show you examples of how you can use the written Word to come against the attacks of the enemy. Let's say that while driving to work one morning, you hear some professor saying over the radio, "One in every five women will develop this disease by the age of forty." That's the time you must say, "It is written—'Surely He shall deliver you from the snare of the fowler *and* from the perilous pestilence'" (Ps. 91:3). If you do this, you are putting up a shield of faith and you are releasing power as you declare that regardless of what the reports of the world say, *your* God *shall* deliver you from every deadly disease!

Here's another example of when and how you can quote the written Word. Suppose for some reason, you are crippled by vivid images in your mind of yourself dying young and leaving your spouse and little ones to fend for themselves. Again, this is the time to speak the Word of God against those fears. Declare, "It is written—'With long life I will satisfy him, and show him My salvation'" (Ps. 91:16).

Maybe you might know of an acquaintance who was killed in a fatal accident. Now, you are fearful that the same thing might happen to you. My friend, the enemy has just shot you with a fiery dart. We do not know what the other person believed. We can only be responsible for our own beliefs and lives. Perhaps your relatives or family members have died from the same illness and the enemy is now attacking you with thoughts that you will also develop diabetes like your father and uncle did, or die from the same heart condition they had.

My friend, if you have been entertaining thoughts like these, NOW is the time to rise up and make this declaration: "A thousand may fall at my side and ten thousand at my right hand, but it shall NOT come near me" (see Ps. 91:7)! For something to happen *at your right hand* means that it has to be really close to you. This means that even if something unfortunate happens to someone close to you, do not allow fear to hold you in its paralyzing grip. Speak forth the written Word of God!

Today's Prayer

Heavenly Father, thank You that You have given me Your written Word to put up a shield of faith and release power to defeat every fear and lying report of the world. Help me to equip myself with the truths from Your Word that will anchor my heart with Your peace and enable me to see victory over the attacks of the enemy. Amen.

Today's Thought

Regardless of what the reports of the world say, I will speak forth the written Word of God and release His power against every attack of the enemy.

DAY 4

SPEAK THE WORD

And since we have the same spirit of faith, according to what is written, "I believed and therefore I spoke," we also believe and therefore speak.

—2 Corinthians 4:13

Beloved, it is not enough for you to merely *know* the Word in your heart. You must *say* it. That's when latent power becomes actual power. When our Lord Jesus was tempted in the wilderness, He did not merely think about Scripture. He spoke it out loud. You can memorize thousands of Scriptures, but if you don't learn to say, "It is written," and release the Word, there will be no power. God's power is there, but it is all lying dormant inside you. The moment you speak it out, it is as if God is speaking. God's Word in *your* mouth is like God speaking. Amen!

Fear is not something you can reason or analyze away. Fear is irrational. There are some fears that come into your life and you can think to yourself, *Come on, what are the chances of that happening?* or *It's so silly to fear this.* But have you noticed that those fears still hang around? We are in a war, my friend, and the only way to defeat fear is to speak the Word of God to whatever fear you have by saying, "It is written."

It is written—"For God has not given us a spirit of fear, but of power and of love and of a sound mind" (2 Tim. 1:7).

I want you to memorize that. It's a powerful verse of Scripture.

Now, I want you to say this out loud: It is written—"For God has not given us a spirit of fear, but of power and of love and of a sound mind." Do you feel the power that comes with saying this aloud?

This is the truth: God has not given us a spirit of fear, but of *power* and of *love* and of *a sound mind*. I don't care what kind of fears you are battling with—fear of growing old, fear of contracting this or that disease, fear of losing your job, fear of failure. Whatever the fear that has come against you, declare, "It is written."

What if the fear comes back? Then say it again! Sometimes, I speak Scriptures over my situation in the morning, in the afternoon, and in the evening. Whenever the fear comes back, I speak the Word of God. If the devil wants a fight, give him one! Give him the sword of the Spirit and he will get the *point* every time. There are many Scriptures you can memorize. Write down the Scriptures that cover the areas of your need, and arm yourself with them!

Today's Prayer

*Father, thank You for the power of Your Word that is
released into my situation when I speak Your Word.
Thank You that You have given me a spirit of power and
of love and of a sound mind. Help me to get more of Your
Word and promises deep into my heart and to boldly speak
them against the enemy and his attacks. Amen.*

Today's Thought

*When I speak the written Word of God, I release the
power of God into my situation.*

DAY 5

RELEASE GOD'S POWER INTO YOUR SITUATION

As He is, so are we in this world.

—1 John 4:17

✥

Let me share with you how Megan, a precious lady from Minnesota, confronted her fears by speaking the Word of God for the area of her need and saw the power of God released in her situation. I'll let her tell you her story:

I was diagnosed with throat and neck cancer. After a series of treatments, I recovered and tests showed that there was no more cancer. However, two years later, the doctors found a mass in my throat again.

At that time, I'd begun watching Joseph Prince on television. He shared a testimony of a woman who had taken hold of 1 John 4:17—"as He is, so are we in this world"—for herself and ended up not needing to have any surgery.

So I took hold of this Scripture for myself as well. My first thought after hearing the doctor's diagnosis was, "As Jesus is, so am I in this world. Since He does not have cancer, then neither do I."

Fear tried to enter my thoughts over the next several days, but I believed and kept declaring 1 John 4:17 as I was being told that I might have cancer again. I was advised to have a biopsy done and was also told that a bilateral tonsillectomy, a procedure to remove the tonsils, would be needed.

As I was being prepped for surgery, I was asked if there was anything I wanted to say. I said, "Yes. When the doctor comes in to do the surgery, she will say that the surgery is not needed and there is no cancer."

And that was exactly what happened! The tonsillectomy was canceled because the biopsy showed that I did not have cancer! When told the good news, I smiled and said, "Thank You, Jesus!"

I have your book, 100 Days of Favor, which has a page that teaches on 1 John 4:17. I keep a bookmark on that page and read it often.

I am continually being set free by the gospel of grace. Thank you, Pastor Prince!

Praise the Lord—what an awesome testimony of the power of the written Word released through our mouths! Beloved, what the Lord did for Megan, He can and will do for you too!

Today's Prayer
Lord Jesus, thank You that Your Word states that as You are, so am I in this world. Thank You that as You are full of peace, health, and strength, so am I in this world. I declare that Your Word is true for every need in my life. Amen.

Today's Thought
I will declare and stand on God's Word that as Jesus is, so am I in this world.

DAY 6

THE POWER OF THE WRITTEN WORD

*For I am not ashamed of the gospel of Christ, for it is
the power of God to salvation for everyone who believes,
for the Jew first and also for the Greek.*

—*Romans 1:16*

Some years ago, I went to Israel with my pastors and we were introduced to a Jewish believer who became our guide. This man, who believes that Jesus is the Messiah, served as a paratrooper in the Israel Defense Forces during the fourth Arab-Israeli war in 1973. He told us how Israel had been taken by surprise when Egyptian and Syrian forces launched a coordinated attack against Israel on Yom Kippur (the Day of Atonement), the holiest day in the Jewish calendar. Israel's enemies were able to sweep in and take over large swathes of territory because many of their soldiers were away from their posts, observing the Day of Atonement. Once they became aware of the attack, our guide was activated to enter enemy ground together with his platoon.

In that platoon, there were five soldiers who had made fun

of him and who had persecuted him for his beliefs before the war. They'd told him that he had betrayed his own people and was no longer fit to be called a Jew because he had accepted Jesus Christ as Messiah. In response, he had told them that if his God were not real, they would see him die. But if Jesus were Lord, he told them, "with your eyes you will see wondrous things" happening to him right before them.

Our guide described how, during the Yom Kippur war, they had entered a forested area when, without warning, they were ambushed with general-purpose machine gun (GPMG) shots being fired all around. The platoon commander in front of him was the first to get hit—he was shot in the head and dropped straight to the ground. As the second-in-command, our guide took over immediately. As he fired a volley of shots, he shouted for some of his men to shoot toward his left and called for another group of them to aim behind some rocks in another direction. But he heard no response at all from his men. When he turned to look for them, he realized that no one was there.

All his men had dived into a trench and he was the only one standing in the open. He walked over and peered into the trench. One of the men motioned for him to jump into the hole with them, screaming, "Come on, you'll die!" Our guide did not heed their cries. Instead, he yelled, "Get out here and fight!"

As he stood there, he suddenly became aware of GPMG bullets flying all around him—so many whizzing past him that they sounded like bees buzzing round his head. His platoon mates, trembling in fear, including the five who had constantly teased him, stared up at him in awe. Then, he realized what was happening to him—in the midst of heavy gunfire, the Lord was protecting him. He was standing exposed in the open with gunfire pounding the surrounding trees, leaves falling all around him. But not a single bullet touched him. He looked down and shouted at them, "With your eyes you see! *Now*, do you believe?"

Not a single bullet touched him. Isn't that amazing?

Our guide told us that he had grown up in a small church. On the pulpit at the front of the sanctuary was a plaque that he always looked at as a child when he got bored with the sermon he was hearing. He kept on reading those words until they entered his spirit and he believed them. Those words were: "A thousand may fall at your side, and ten thousand at your right hand; *but* it shall not come near you."

He grew up believing that regardless of who fell around him, it would never happen to him. In fact, as the bullets tore past him, he shared with us that he did not fear even for a moment that any of the bullets would hit him.

I pray that the Scripture our guide meditated on will

guard your heart, keep you Christ-occupied, and in faith. Whatever the danger is, *it shall not come near you!* Be strengthened by His promise to you and start walking in the power and authority of God's Word today.

Today's Prayer

Father God, thank You that no matter what anyone says or what I see and hear, Your Word is true and I will stand upon it. Thank You that Your wondrous power is demonstrated as I believe and speak Your Word. I declare that whatever the danger is, whether it is disease, disasters, or terrorist attacks, it shall not come near me and my loved ones. Amen.

Today's Thought

I will declare and fill my heart with the promises of Psalm 91, and walk in the power and authority of God's Word.

STAND UPON GOD'S PROMISES

His divine power has given to us all things that pertain to life and godliness, through the knowledge of Him who called us by glory and virtue, by which have been given to us exceedingly great and precious promises, that through these you may be partakers of the divine nature.

—2 Peter 1:3–4

In the previous reading, I recounted the story of how our Jewish guide in Israel was miraculously protected during the fourth Arab-Israeli war in 1973. He grew up believing the written Word—"A thousand may fall at your side, and ten thousand at your right hand; *but* it shall not come near you."

In contrast, he told us about a friend in the army who had gone to the Israeli military academy together with him. During the Yom Kippur war, his friend told him this: "I've got a feeling that I won't make it through this war. I just feel I'm going to die in this war." Although our guide told him not to say such things, his friend continued. He believed he would die in the war as much as our guide believed that he would not. Sadly, this friend was indeed killed during the war.

The devil is known as "the accuser of our brethren" (Rev. 12:10). He will always try to keep you self-occupied and in fear. God wants you Christ-occupied and in faith! You might have a friend of the same age who perhaps died suddenly from an illness even though he or she had seemed healthier than you. The devil will try to plant fears in your heart that you are next. By now, you know what to do. Take up your shield of faith and declare, "It is written—'A thousand may fall at your side, and ten thousand at your right hand; but it shall not come near you.'" Whatever "it" may be—cancer, disease, accidents, terrorist attacks—it shall not come near you! When you board a plane, that plane has no choice but to land safely because YOU are on board, Amen!

Beloved, the Lord Jesus sacrificed His life on the cross so that you can stand upon His promises and claim them for *your* life. They are all fully paid for by the blood of Jesus, and the Father will see to it that you enjoy them! If you do not know what promises to claim, can I encourage you to start with the many promises listed in Psalm 91? Memorize Psalm 91 and when you are under attack, quote it the way our Lord Jesus quoted Scripture. Meditate on Psalm 91 and allow yourself to be fortified by this prayer of protection. There is such a power and authority that comes with quoting the pure and unadulterated written Word of God, and I invite you to start walking in that power and authority today!

Today's Prayer

Father in heaven, thank You for giving me Your exceedingly great and precious promises to stand upon and claim for my life. Thank You that I can meditate on Psalm 91 and be fortified by this prayer of protection. I will stand upon Your promises and walk in the power and authority of Your Word. Amen.

Today's Thought

I have been given the exceedingly great and precious promises of God to stand upon, and I will walk in the power and authority of His Word as I proclaim it.

SECTION VII

DWELL SAFELY IN CHRIST, YOUR REFUGE

Because you have made the LORD, who is my refuge,
Even the Most High, your dwelling place,
No evil shall befall you,
Nor shall any plague come near your dwelling.
                                    —Psalm 91:9–10

NO EVIL SHALL
BEFALL YOU

*Because you have made the LORD, who is my refuge,
even the Most High, your dwelling place, no evil shall
befall you, nor shall any plague come near your dwelling.*
—Psalm 91:9–10

When I was a student, I took on a part-time job in a factory that manufactured refrigerators. Like any teenager, I had just wanted to earn some extra pocket money. It wasn't a complicated job. I was part of an assembly line and all I had to do was use an electric drill to create an opening and to fasten a condenser securely onto the back of each refrigerator. I would be buzzing away on the power drill all day, earning my keep.

At that time, I had the habit of carrying a small booklet around with me. It was my little booklet of Bible memory verses, and I would read from it and speak the Word of God three times a day. During that period, there was one particular verse in Psalm 91 that I would confess every day: "No evil shall befall you, nor shall any plague come near your dwelling" (Ps. 91:10). It was my daily confession in the morning

before I left for work, and during my break times, my coworkers would see me sitting in some corner, confessing this verse.
It was a very powerful revelation for me, and I really wanted
His Word, and in particular this truth of God's protection, to
drop into my heart.

One day, as I was assembling yet another refrigerator, I
lost control of the power drill. It somehow slipped out of my
hands and the drill went straight toward my stomach. Everything happened really quickly. The power drill, which was
spinning at full force, hit my stomach…and it just bounced
off. Some of the workers there who saw what had happened
ran over, concerned for me. It was then that I realized I was
completely unharmed!

The only thing that came to mind at that moment was
the Scripture I had been meditating on. That day, the verse,
"No evil shall befall you, nor shall any plague come near your
dwelling" came alive for me. I give thanks for the Lord's divine
protection over my life when I was a teenager. Don't you just
love our wonderful and beautiful Savior! As you meditate on
and declare His promises in His Word, I believe you'll also see
His saving and delivering power working on your behalf.

Today's Prayer

*Lord Jesus, thank You for being my refuge and my
dwelling place. I declare that as I come under
Your wings of protection, no evil shall befall me,
nor shall any plague come near my dwelling.
I rest in Your wonderful love. Amen.*

Today's Thought

*Because I have made the Lord my refuge and
dwelling place, no evil shall befall me, nor shall any
plague come near my dwelling.*

JESUS, YOUR CITY OF REFUGE

Then said Jesus, Father, forgive them;
for they know not what they do.

—*Luke 23:34 KJV*

⌘

There is a teaching on the cities of refuge from the Old Testament that I believe will encourage you to take the Lord as your refuge and protector and run to Him.

The Lord told Joshua that when the children of Israel entered the land of Canaan, they were to designate six cities of refuge. Back in those days, if someone unintentionally killed a person, the closest relative of the deceased had the legal right to avenge him. However, in His mercy, God appointed six cities and said, "Anyone who kills another person accidentally and unintentionally can run to one of these cities; they will be places of refuge from relatives seeking revenge for the person who was killed" (Josh. 20:3 NLT).

The cities of refuge were designed for people who had committed unintentional manslaughter, not for those who had carried out premeditated homicide. Deuteronomy 19 explains this, stating: "If someone kills another person unintentionally, without previous hostility…the slayer may flee to one of the cities of refuge to live in safety" (vv. 4–5 NLT).

The six cities of refuge are also a beautiful picture of our Lord Jesus, hidden for us to unveil. They are shadows that point to the substance—our Lord and Savior, Jesus Christ. In the Old Testament, He is concealed. In the New Testament, He is revealed.

At the cross, our Lord Jesus put all our sins, including the sin of crucifying Him, under the category of "unintentional" when He prayed, "Father, forgive them; for they know not what they do" (Luke 23:34 KJV). He was not just referring to Israel or the Romans; all *our* sins nailed Jesus to the cross. He chose the nails and offered us complete forgiveness. Can you see how good and merciful our God is?

Today, if you call upon the name of Jesus, you are qualified to run to Him and take Him as your city of refuge. Jesus is your city of refuge, and when you run to Him for refuge, the one seeking revenge (a picture of the devil) no longer has power over you. My friend, we were all sinners and the wages of sin is death (see Rom. 6:23). Before the cross, the devil had the legal right to put a death sentence over your head because of your sins. But the good news of the gospel is that Jesus took that death sentence at the cross, and in Christ we can receive His forgiveness and His protection. Hallelujah!

Today's Prayer

Lord Jesus, I call upon Your name and thank You that my family and I can take You as our city of refuge. Thank You that the devil's legal right to put a death sentence over my head was wiped out when You took all my sins at the cross. I declare that I have received Your forgiveness and am free to enjoy Your protection. Amen.

Today's Thought

Because Jesus is my city of refuge, I have received His forgiveness and have the legal right to walk in His protection.

THE GOOD SHEPHERD

He will protect His flock like a shepherd,
He will gather the lambs in His arm, He will carry
them in His bosom; He will gently and carefully
lead those nursing their young.

—Isaiah 40:11 AMP

❧

I want to show you how there are no insignificant details in the Bible by uncovering hidden truths concealed in the names of the six cities of refuge that I mentioned in the previous reading. Read along with me and let's see what the Lord has for us: "So they appointed **Kedesh** in Galilee, in the mountains of Naphtali, **Shechem** in the mountains of Ephraim, and **Kirjath Arba** (which is Hebron) in the mountains of Judah. And on the other side of the Jordan, by Jericho eastward, they assigned **Bezer** in the wilderness on the plain, from the tribe of Reuben, **Ramoth** in Gilead, from the tribe of Gad, and **Golan** in Bashan, from the tribe of Manasseh" (Josh. 20:7–8, boldface mine).

Let me give you the meaning of the names in order of their appearance. *Kedesh* means holy place or sanctuary.[14] In the cities of refuge, people sought asylum in the sanctuaries.

Then we have *Shechem*, which means shoulder.[15] Shechem, by the way, is where Jacob's well is. Our Lord Jesus met the woman at the well in Shechem. Joseph was buried in Shechem and his tomb is still there. Next, we have Kirjath Arba, which is Hebron. *Hebron* means friendship or fellowship,[16] and is the place where Abraham and Sarah were buried. Then, on the east side of the Jordan River, we have *Bezer*, which means fortress,[17] followed by *Ramoth*, which means heights or highly exalted.[18] We end with *Golan*, which means rejoicing or joy.[19]

Now, let's put these names together to see the message for us: You can find sanctuary (Kedesh) on the Lord's strong shoulders (Shechem), which He offers in fellowship (Hebron). He is our fortress (Bezer) and He highly exalts (Ramoth) us above all our troubles with great rejoicing (Golan).

Hallelujah, all praise and glory to the Name above all names! The names paint a stunning picture of our Lord Jesus, stooping down to where we are, and offering His stronger shoulders to us when we are fearful and weary. What a beautiful picture of the Good Shepherd rescuing His lost sheep!

Beloved, when we have failed and are completely worn out by the fights of life, He offers His shoulders in fellowship. He is our sanctuary. He is our holy place, where we are set apart from the world. When we respond to His desire for fellowship and climb on His broad shoulders, He lifts us up.

Today's Prayer

*Beloved Lord Jesus, thank You that You are my Good
Shepherd and I can find sanctuary on Your strong shoulders
and in fellowshipping with You. Thank You that You
are my fortress and holy place, and You highly exalt me
above all my troubles. I greatly rejoice that as my Shepherd,
You lead, protect, and lift me up when I am
worn out and weak. Amen.*

Today's Thought

*I can find sanctuary on my Good Shepherd's strong
shoulders and in the intimacy of His fellowship. He exalts
me above all my troubles with great rejoicing.*

CONSENT TO BE RESCUED

"What man of you, having a hundred sheep,
if he loses one of them, does not leave the ninety-nine
in the wilderness, and go after the one which is lost until
he finds it? And when he has found it, he lays it on his
shoulders, rejoicing. And when he comes home,
he calls together his friends and neighbors,
saying to them, 'Rejoice with me, for I have
found my sheep which was lost!'"

—Luke 15:4–6

Do you remember the parable of the lost sheep Jesus told in Luke 15? When the shepherd found the lost sheep, he lifted it up and laid it upon his strong shoulders. What did the sheep do? Nothing. It just *consented to be rescued* by the shepherd. Jesus calls this consent on the part of the sheep "repentance"—"there will be more joy in heaven over one sinner who **repents** than over ninety-nine just persons who need no **repentance**" (Luke 15:7, boldface mine).

That is what God invites us to do today—to consent to be protected. He wants us to be on His shoulders, in the safety of

Himself as our impenetrable fortress. In this place, no predator can attack His sheep. On His shoulders, you are highly exalted above all your troubles, above all danger, all attacks, and far above all principalities and powers. Yes, far above Satan, above all the powers of darkness and the snare of the fowler. On His shoulders, you are far above every sickness, disease, and every name that is named. What a great place to be!

And does the Lord do this grudgingly? Absolutely not. The Bible tells us that the shepherd lays the sheep on his shoulders "rejoicing" (Luke 15:5). Our Lord rescues us with great joy in His heart and a big smile on His face.

Beloved, the safest place you can be today is on His shoulders. Jesus is your city of refuge. In your day of trouble, run to Him! I pray you'll anchor your heart on the wonderful verse that encapsulates this: "The beloved of the LORD shall dwell in safety by Him, *who* shelters him all the day long; and he shall dwell between His shoulders" (Deut. 33:12). When you make the Lord your refuge and dwelling place, you shall dwell safely in Him and no evil shall befall you, nor shall any plague come near your dwelling!

Today's Prayer

Abba, Father, thank You for Your unfailing and unshakable love for me. Today, I consent to come under Your wings of protection. I consent to be carried on the shoulders of my Lord Jesus, my Good Shepherd. Thank You that on His shoulders, I am above all danger, all attacks, and far above all principalities and powers. I declare that in Jesus I am in the safest place in the universe. Amen.

Today's Thought

The safest place I can be today is on the shoulders of my Good Shepherd. I gladly consent to be protected by Him and carried on His strong shoulders, where I am above all danger, all attacks, and far above the powers of darkness.

THE LOCAL CHURCH AS A PLACE OF REFUGE

"For where two or three are gathered together in My name, I am there in the midst of them."

—*Matthew 18:20*

Over the past three readings, we've looked at how the Old Testament cities of refuge reveal a beautiful picture of Christ as our protection. Now let me show you another type hidden in the teaching on the cities of refuge, and that is the picture of the local church. The six cities are scattered across the land so a person can flee to the nearest one to take refuge. It is a picture of local churches scattered all around the world. The local church, my friend, is a place of refuge. The church is not man's idea; it is God's idea. It is a place where all the guilty, where all who are suffering from condemnation, and where those who are being pursued can come and take refuge. You see, it is not God's heart for you to take this journey of faith on your own. Certainly, you can learn a lot by reading books or watching sermons online, but God's heart is for you to be part of a *community* of faith.

In the Father's house, people experience healing, breakthroughs, protection, and other blessings. God the Father raised Jesus from the dead and seated Him at His right hand in the heavenly places, "far above all principality and power and might and dominion, and every name that is named" (Eph. 1:21). This means that Jesus is far above all sicknesses, all diseases, all terror, all snares, all cancers, all depression, and all addictions. Amen!

We all agree that our Lord is above every name, but on this earth, where does this power and dominion reside? The apostle Paul declares, "And He put all *things* under His feet, and gave Him *to be* head over all *things* to the church, which is His body, the fullness of Him who fills all in all" (Eph. 1:22–23). Where is this power today in our broken and fallen world? It is found in the church! His power, His authority, and His fullness are all found in the church—our city of refuge where we can run to and find divine protection!

Today's Prayer

Father God, thank You that Your heart for me is to be a part of a local church, which is the body of Christ, where we gather in His name and He is in our midst. Thank You that His power, His authority, and His fullness are found in and made available to me in the church. Amen.

Today's Thought

God's heart for me is to be a part of a community of faith, which is the body of Christ, where I find His power, His authority, and the fullness of His divine protection.

FIND RESTORATION
IN THE CHURCH

Those who are planted in the house of the LORD shall
flourish in the courts of our God. They shall still bear
fruit in old age; they shall be fresh and flourishing,
to declare that the LORD is upright; He is my rock,
and there is no unrighteousness in Him.

—*Psalm 92:13–15*

I received this praise report from a couple who attends our Grace Revolution Church in Dallas, Texas. It's a beautiful example of how we walk in His protection and restoration as we are planted in the house of God. This couple shared with me how their marriage had gone through a very challenging period, and how the church and the pastoral leadership had helped them through that difficult time.

It took us some time to realize that we needed to focus
more on Christ rather than on ourselves and on our prob-
lems. What ultimately saved our relationship was focus-
ing vertically on our Lord Jesus and not horizontally on
each other. We were declaring, "I am the righteousness of

God in Christ Jesus," which gave us a sense of how much God loves us and wants us blessed. Knowing that we are the righteousness of God through Christ is what healed our broken marriage.

Being able to rest in all that Jesus has done, and being able to hear and meditate on the Word, has been the best thing for us. He truly is the vine and we are the branches. We now know that in every situation and circumstance, Christ is supplying our every need. He is the vine that will keep us supplied and where we need to be.

Knowing that "if it matters to me, it matters to God" was the last piece of the puzzle. We learned that there is no matter too small or too inconsequential to the Lord. Neither is there anything too big for Him to tackle for us.

Dear reader, can you see how important it is to be planted in a local church? In this couple's case, being in a church that preached the truth of the gospel and having the wise counsel of leaders who walked the journey with them saved their marriage.

And can you sense their joy in knowing that the Lord Jesus is their vine who supplies their every need, and to whom nothing is too big or too small for them to bring? Read today's verses from Psalm 92. Bearing fruit in old age speaks of preservation, protection, and long life. God wants you not only to have long life, but to have quality of life and still be strong, healthy, and fruitful in your old age. And the way to have all of that is to be *planted* in the house of the Lord. Beloved, if you are not regularly attending a local church, I want to encourage you to be planted in one. As you do so, may you, your career, your marriage, and your household flourish in every way!

Today's Prayer

Lord Jesus, thank You that You are the head over the church as well as the vine who supplies every need that I have. Help me to be planted in Your house, and to be surrounded by leaders and like-minded believers who will cause me to bear fruit and flourish in every area of my life. Amen.

Today's Thought

As I am planted in the house of the Lord, quality of life, strength, health, and fruitfulness are mine to walk in.

FIND PROTECTION
IN THE CHURCH

And let us not neglect our meeting together, as some
people do, but encourage one another, especially now
that the day of his return is drawing near.
—*Hebrews 10:25* NLT

The brother in the previous reading who attends Grace Revolution Church in Dallas also shared with me another precious testimony of how the Lord had protected him and his wife from the tragic terrorist attacks that took place in Paris:

To celebrate our anniversary on November 10, 2015,
I wanted to do something very special. My wife enjoys
cooking and baking, and loves French cuisine. We had
been talking about traveling to Europe and I thought
this would be a good time for us to travel to Paris to cel-
ebrate our anniversary. I had set up a trip leaving on the
Wednesday and returning on the Sunday of that week.

However, I forgot Pastor Prince's Grace Revolution
Tour was taking place in Dallas during the same week-
end. Because I was trying to keep the trip a secret, my

wife didn't know to remind me either! But when I told her my plan three weeks early, she quickly pointed out my oversight and I rescheduled the trip for springtime. I was disappointed at that time about not getting to go on the trip.

We now know that the terrorist attack in Paris started on the afternoon of the Friday I'd planned for us to be there. Had we gone to Paris as I had originally planned, we would have been there during the attack.

Pastor Prince had been preaching on divine protection quite a bit, especially over the year before. We had been hearing from Pastor Prince not to take our protection for granted, and had started sharing with our boys about how we are protected by our Father. We had begun praying with them to thank the Lord for His protection over our lives. We both felt that we had experienced God's "right place, right time" protection.

I'm not sure how close we would have been to the horrible terror acts had we gone on the trip, but I do know that God's grace kept us thousands of miles out of harm's way. We were protected, enjoying that time with our family, singing praises to God with the church's worship team, and learning more about grace from Pastor Prince in Dallas!

Do you see, dear reader, how we can learn about and be led to walk in God's divine protection over our lives when we take His Word seriously and are planted in a local church? In every way our lives and our marriages will be preserved, protected, and flourishing.

Today's Prayer
Father, thank You that You have the power and the know-how to keep me away from all that would harm me. Thank You for leading me to a local church where I can be equipped with Your Word and grow in Your grace. Help me to always experience Your right place, right time protection. Amen.

Today's Thought
As I keep hearing preaching on and see myself under the Father's protection, my life, family, career, and ministry cannot help but be preserved, protected, and full of good fruit.

GOD IS YOUR REFUGE FROM EVIL

Because thou hast made the LORD, which is my refuge,
even the most High, thy habitation; there shall
no evil befall thee, neither shall any plague
come nigh thy dwelling.

—*Psalm 91:9–10 KJV*

Isn't the above passage beautiful in the King James Version? You can make the Lord your *habitation*. First John 4:16 says, "God is love, and he who abides in love abides in God, and God in him." The more you stay in His love, the more God Himself becomes your dwelling place. No evil shall befall you and no plague shall come near your dwelling. And as you make Him your dwelling place, He protects your dwelling. No plague shall even come near your home! In another psalm, it is written, "God *is* our refuge and strength, a very present help in trouble" (Ps. 46:1). As we make the Lord our city of refuge and allow Him to put us upon His shoulders, He becomes our "very present help" even if we encounter trouble.

Iris from Australia experienced God's protection for

herself when a cyclone hit the area she lived in. Read her testimony here:

> *A mini cyclone hit our street and the surrounding area recently. As I huddled in the hallway with my husband and our cat, I declared, "Thank You, Jesus, that You are the calm in the storm!"*
>
> *When the wind stopped, we went outside and saw a lot of fallen trees on the road. The trees in our street were huge and as tall as thirty meters. As a result, many cars were crushed by the trees and some houses were also damaged. My husband's work car was damaged slightly but our family car was left unscathed. And praise the Lord no one was injured!*
>
> *As the damaged trees were being cut down across the road, I realized something. The path of the wind had cut through a few properties across the road and when it came near our house, it stopped completely! It did not come near us and our house was completely undamaged.*
>
> *Everyone in our street was so surprised that the big tree in our backyard was untouched and that we had no cleanup of our own to do. Praise Jesus! He is the calm, peace, and protection I need!*

Wow, praise the Lord! I love this testimony—when the

Lord Himself is your refuge and your protection, even cyclones have to stop in their tracks when they come near you!

Today's Prayer
Heavenly Father, thank You for Your love in which I can abide and rest. Thank You that You are my habitation and dwelling place, where no evil may befall me and no plague can come near me. I declare that You are my very present help in times of trouble. Amen.

Today's Thought
Because I have made the Lord my habitation and dwelling place, He is my very present help when I encounter trouble.

DAY 9

THE LORD OUR REFUGE

It is better to trust in the LORD than to
put confidence in man.

—*Psalm 118:8*

The prayer of protection declares, "Because **you** have made the LORD, *who is* my refuge, *even* the Most High, **your** dwelling place, no evil shall befall **you**" (Ps. 91:9–10, boldface mine). The Word of God does not say that no evil shall befall "the world." It says that no evil shall befall *you.* Verse 10 goes on to say, "nor shall any plague come near your dwelling," and that includes your family. Beloved, let this Scripture strengthen and anchor your heart. Because you have made the Lord your refuge, no plague will come near your dwelling. Protection from strains of viruses that science does not yet have a cure for—Ebola, Zika, or AIDS—is God's promise to you and your household!

Have you made the Lord your refuge? Today's Scripture says, "*It is* better to trust in the LORD than to put confidence in man." Interestingly, the Hebrew word for "trust" is *chacah*, which is the root word for "refuge" in Psalm 91.[20]

In other words, to make the Lord your refuge is to trust Him in all things. Trust Him with your plans, with your life, and with your family. Trust Him for His leading and wisdom. Confide in Him. Our Lord Jesus is not distant; He is not a Savior who is far away. He is so personal…so near you. There is safety and protection when we draw near to Him and dwell in His sweet presence, His Word, and His house.

As I said at the beginning of this book, in the natural, the world is getting darker and darker. But don't look around you and be distressed. Don't look inside you and be depressed. Look to the Lord Jesus and be completely at rest! As children of the Most High, let's pray today's prayer together right now!

Today's Prayer

Father, I thank You for Psalm 91. I thank You that I am in Christ. I live in that realm where no evil—no economic calamities and upheavals—shall befall me, and no plague shall come near my dwelling. YOU are my refuge and my hiding place, and I thank You that with long life, You satisfy me. Thank You, Father, for giving up Your Son to die at Calvary so that today, I can be safe and secure in the secret place of the Most High. As Christ is, so am I in this world. As Christ is seated at Your right hand, far above every principality and every power, SO AM I! Amen.

Today's Thought

There is safety and protection when I draw near to God and trust Him in all things.

SECTION VIII

ACTIVATING HIS ANGELS

For He shall give His angels charge over you,
To keep you in all your ways.
In their hands they shall bear you up,
Lest you dash your foot against a stone.

—*Psalm 91:11–12*

MORE WITH US THAN AGAINST US

"Do not fear, for those who are with us are more than those who are with them."

—*2 Kings 6:16*

In the days of the prophet Elisha, the king of Syria seized upon an opportunity to capture Elisha who was in the city of Dothan. He mobilized a great army with many chariots and horses to surround the city one night. He wasn't prepared to take any risk of the prophet escaping.

Early the next morning in Dothan, when Elisha's servant went outside, he saw troops, horses, and chariots everywhere. He and Elisha were completely surrounded by enemy forces intent on killing them. The servant flew into a state of panic and cried out to Elisha, "Alas, my master! What shall we do?" (2 Kings 6:15).

Put yourself in the shoes of Elisha's servant. You (and I) would probably have been filled with fear too. But here's where I want you to pay close attention, because there is a powerful truth I want you to catch. Without faltering, Elisha calmly told his servant, "Do not fear, for those who *are* with us *are* more than those who *are* with them" (2 Kings 6:16).

I can just imagine how the servant must have felt. There was absolutely no logic in what Elisha had just said. There were just the two of them against a whole army! Had his master gone mad?

Before the servant could work himself into an even greater panic, Elisha prayed a simple prayer: "LORD, I pray, open his eyes that he may see" (2 Kings 6:17). And the Lord opened the eyes of the servant. Then he saw that the hillside all around them was filled with blindingly magnificent horses and chariots of fire. God's army of angels was flanking them on every side, ablaze with the glory, beauty, and majesty of the Most High. As the servant marveled, he realized that the Syrian forces were utterly dwarfed by the angelic army.

Why had the young servant been fearful while Elisha was fearless? The answer is this: They saw different things. The young man saw the great Syrian army. But Elisha saw an *even greater* angelic army on chariots of fire. Elisha had *spiritual insight*.

My dear reader, would you commit the above Scripture to heart? If you are in a constant fight with fear, meditate on this Scripture and fortify your heart with this promise. Whether you find yourself besieged by debts, attacked by what doctors call a terminal illness, or constantly anxious over the safety of your children, remember this powerful verse. The God of angelic armies is with you. No weapon formed against you shall prosper (see Isa. 54:17)!

Today's Prayer

Father God, open my eyes that I may see Your army of angels surrounding me on every side on horses and in chariots of fire, ablaze with glory. Thank You that no matter how big the cause for fear, those who are with me are greater than those who are against me. I declare that no weapon formed against me shall prosper. Amen.

Today's Thought

No matter what I face, I will not fear, for those who are with me—God's army of angels—are more than those who are against me.

HE GIVES HIS ANGELS CHARGE OVER YOU

For He shall give His angels charge over you,
to keep you in all your ways. In their hands
they shall bear you up, lest you dash
your foot against a stone.

—Psalm 91:11–12

✺

What a wonderful promise we have in the above passage! In the same way the angels surrounded Elisha and his servant and protected them, they are surrounding us and protecting us today, *because God has given them charge over us to protect us*! When we choose to make Him our habitation, He charges His angels to watch over us and to surround us with His divine protection.

Now, did you know that Psalm 91:11–12 was quoted by the devil when he tried to tempt our Lord Jesus? He brought our Lord to the pinnacle of the temple and said to Him, "If You are the Son of God, throw Yourself down. For it is written: 'He shall give His angels charge over you,' and, 'In *their* hands they shall bear you up, lest you dash your foot against a stone.'" To this Jesus replied, "It is written again, 'You shall not tempt the LORD your God'" (Matt. 4:5–7).

The temptation of our Lord Jesus in the wilderness is the only instance in the Bible where the devil is recorded quoting Scripture. But the devil deliberately misquoted verse 11. The devil misquotes the Bible because he is the father of lies. Verse 11 actually reads (boldface mine): "For He shall give His angels charge over you, **to keep you in all your ways**."

I asked the Lord why the devil left out the words "to keep you in all your ways" and He directed me to Proverbs 3:6–7 (boldface mine), which says: "**In all your ways** acknowledge Him, and He shall direct your paths. Do not be wise in your own eyes; fear the LORD and depart from evil."

You see, the devil didn't want to say the words "to keep you in all your ways" because that would be tantamount to reminding believers of Proverbs 3:6–7—to acknowledge God in all our ways. So he conveniently left out that whole portion. But praise the Lord, we know that *this* is what the Lord has promised: "For He shall give His angels charge over you, **to keep you in all your ways**" (boldface mine). Our part is to simply acknowledge Him in all our ways, and He shall direct our paths, protecting us along the way!

Today's Prayer

*Father in heaven, thank You that as I make You my
habitation, You give Your angels charge over me to protect
me in all my ways. I humble myself before You and choose
to acknowledge You in all that I do. I believe that You
shall direct my paths and protect me from every
evil today and in the days ahead. Amen.*

Today's Thought

*God has charged His angels to protect and keep
me in all my ways, as I acknowledge Him in
all that I set out to do.*

EXERCISE WISDOM AND WALK IN PROTECTION

Don't forget to show hospitality to strangers,
for some who have done this have entertained
angels without realizing it!

—*Hebrews 13:2* NLT

In the previous reading, if you look carefully at the Scriptures that Satan used to try to get our Lord Jesus to throw Himself down from the pinnacle of the temple, you will find that it has nothing to do with endangering yourself to test God's protection. Psalm 91:11–12 is not encouraging you to throw yourself in harm's way. It is saying that as you go about the course of your daily life, "in all your ways" the Lord will protect you. The Hebrew word for "ways" in verse 11 shows this clearly—it is the word *derek*, which means path, road, or journey.[21]

As you go about your daily path, there are times when the enemy may have put snares ahead of you that you are unaware of. But God will give His angels charge over you, to go ahead of you to protect you from those snares. It doesn't mean that you should go and do something foolish and harmful to yourself to test God's protection! Even as we trust the Lord for His divine protection, let's exercise wisdom as well.

You may be familiar with Mark 16:18, which says, "If they drink anything deadly, it will by no means hurt them." Now, if someone challenges you to drink poison and you willfully drink it to show that it will not hurt you, that's just being foolish. Psalm 91:11 is talking about the paths you take as part of your normal life. Drinking poison intentionally is certainly not part of your normal life. What Mark 16:18 is saying is that should you drink something harmful without realizing it in the course of your day, the Lord will protect you from being harmed!

I have a missionary friend who told me how someone had tried to poison him while he was in the mission field. In the end, the person became a believer in the Lord Jesus because he saw the missionary innocently drinking the entire glass of poison—and suffering no ill effects. *That's* how Mark 16:18 applies!

And I hope you realize that God's protection does not always have to come in the form of spectacular angelic interventions. I believe that every day, His protection over us is so supernaturally natural that many of us don't even realize that we have been protected. Perhaps as you were stepping off the curb, you felt something hold or pull you back, and right then, a car sped past you. What do you think held or pulled you back? It may well have been an angel, not necessarily spectacularly, but supernaturally protecting you!

Today's Prayer

Lord Jesus, thank You that Your angels protect me in all my ways as I go about the course of my daily life. Help me to walk in wisdom. I ask and thank You for Your supernaturally natural protection over me and my loved ones every day. Amen.

Today's Thought

Angelic protection covers me in all my ways as I go about the course of my daily life and walk in the Lord's wisdom.

ANGELS ALL AROUND YOU

*Bless the LORD, you His angels, who **excel in strength**,*
*who do His word, **heeding the voice of His word**.*
Bless the LORD, all you His hosts, you ministers
of His, who do His pleasure.
—*Psalm 103:20–21 (boldface mine)*

Some people have the impression that angels look like little babies dressed in white togas, flying about with bows and arrows. The passage above tells us they are strong—they "excel in strength." Do you know how strong angels can be? When Sennacherib, the evil king of Assyria, laid a siege around Jerusalem, Hezekiah prayed to the Lord and the Lord sent one angel to the Assyrian camp. Just one angel. In one night, the Bible tells us that "the angel of the LORD went out to the Assyrian camp and killed 185,000 Assyrian soldiers" (2 Kings 19:35 NLT).

Here's something else about angels: they "do His word." They do not operate outside the boundaries of God's Word. And we have seen in Psalm 91:11–12 that the Lord has given His angels charge over us. The Amplified Classic version says that His angels will "**accompany** *and* **defend** *and* **preserve** you in all your ways" (boldface mine). I don't know about you but that gives me such assurance that I am covered under His wings of refuge and protection!

The Word of God also tells us that when the archangel Lucifer fell, one-third of the angels fell with him. That means that two-thirds of the angels are still on God's side! Hebrews 12:22 tells us of an "innumerable company of angels." There are so many angels that they cannot be numbered. We may not be able to see them, but they are all around us, ministering for us. So don't be one of those believers who are more conscious of demons than angels. Remember, *those who are with us are more than those who are with them* (see 2 Kings 6:16)!

In the Garden of Gethsemane, when the Roman soldiers came to arrest our Lord, He said, "Do you suppose that I cannot appeal to My Father, and He will immediately provide Me with more than twelve legions of angels?" (Matt. 26:53 AMPC). According to the Amplified translation, twelve legions is more than 80,000 angels! All Jesus had to do was pray and those angels would have been activated. But He did not do so because He had already chosen to go to the cross and to die the death that we deserved.

He gave up His protection so that today, you and I can claim all the promises of His protection. And as joint heirs with Christ (see Rom. 8:17), each one of us can summon twelve legions of angels! May you be encouraged as you see His desire to protect you as well as His provision of angelic protection over your life.

Today's Prayer

Father, thank You for the innumerable angels who are around me, ministering for me, obeying Your Word to defend and preserve me in all my ways. Thank You that Jesus gave up His protection so that I can claim all the promises of His protection. As a joint heir with Christ, I believe there are legions of angels ready to protect me. Amen.

Today's Thought

I may not see them, but innumerable angels are around me, ministering for me, because Jesus paid the price for me to have such protection.

DAY 5

WORSHIP ACTIVATES ANGELS

*The angel of the LORD encamps all around those
who fear Him, and delivers them.*

—*Psalm 34:7*

Beloved, we have a resource that is greater than any attack the devil can launch against us. Would you like to know how you can activate angels in your life?

The most important key is *worship*. As you offer your praise to the Lord, the passage above tells us that's when angels are most active. Our Lord Jesus defined "fear" as "worship" for us. When Satan tempted Him in the wilderness, Jesus responded by quoting from Deuteronomy 6:13, which says, "You shall fear the LORD your God." But He changed the word "fear" to "worship" and said to the devil, "For it is written, 'You shall **worship** the LORD your God'" (Matt. 4:10, boldface mine).

Beloved, when you worship the Lord, His angels camp all around you, surrounding you to deliver you. If you are going through a difficult period in your life and are fearful, choose to worship Him. Fear fills our hearts when we are occupied with ourselves, but when we worship the Lord, we become occupied with Him, His beauty, and His goodness, and His angels surround us like a protective shield.

My ministry receives praise reports from people all over the world who, upon encountering His love for them personally through the preaching of the gospel, go on to be conscious of and full of thanksgiving for His goodness and grace upon their lives. Let me share with you a praise report from Sophia (who lives in Georgia, US), who's also experienced the Lord's intervention and protection.

Today, I read your Daily Grace Inspiration titled God's Angels Are Watching Over You, *and was really encouraged. I recall an incident when my daughter and I were driving down the road behind an eighteen-wheeler when a vintage-looking car suddenly tried to get between our vehicle and the truck. I thought, "Why are you—" Right then, I heard a voice inside speak to me, asking me to be quiet. So I let the car squeeze in front of us. Immediately after I let the car in, one tire of the eighteen-wheeler blew. Surprisingly, the vintage car stayed in front of my car, taking the full impact of all the flying pieces of the exploded tire.*

Once there were no more tire pieces coming from the truck, the vintage car returned to the left side of the road and drove off quickly. It then dawned on me that perhaps the driver of this car was an angel of the Lord. I was so encouraged to know that God protects us in these days and times!

Amen! When God gives His angels charge over you, they go ahead of you to guard and protect you from all sorts of danger. And yes, they may even choose to travel in vintage cars. Hebrews 13:2 says, "Be not forgetful to entertain strangers: for thereby some have entertained angels unawares" (KJV).

Today's Prayer
Lord Jesus, thank You that when I worship You in Your beauty and goodness, Your angels surround me like a protective shield. Thank You that they camp around my loved ones and me, and go before us to guard and protect us from all sorts of danger. May I always see Your love and grace toward me and worship You. Amen.

Today's Thought
When I worship the Lord, His angels camp all around me, surrounding me to deliver me.

ANGELS HEED THE VOICE OF HIS WORD

As I was praying, Gabriel, whom I had seen in the earlier vision, came swiftly to me at the time of the evening sacrifice. He explained to me, "Daniel, I have come here to give you insight and understanding. The moment you began praying, a command was given. And now I am here to tell you what it was, for you are very precious to God."

—Daniel 9:21–23 NLT

The next key that I want to share with you about activating God's angels is the importance of speaking or declaring the Word of God. Psalm 103:20 tells us that angels heed "the **voice of His word**" (boldface mine).

Who gives voice to God's Word? YOU do. Every time you quote Scriptures out loud, you are giving voice to His Word, and angels will respond. When you say, "Father, I thank You that no evil shall befall me today, nor shall any plague or disease come near my dwelling," angels harken to the voice of the Word of God being spoken. Angels cannot read your mind—so speak forth His Word!

I want to encourage you to study the Word of God and memorize a few verses. When you feel swamped by fear, learn to speak out God's Word. God's power lies dormant until you speak it forth. When you do, it becomes real and powerful in your situation and comes against whatever you might be facing.

Hebrews 1:14 says that God's angels are "all ministering spirits sent forth to minister **for** those who will inherit salvation" (boldface mine). Notice that it doesn't say "minister to" but "minister for" those who will inherit salvation (that refers to children of God—you and me). That's an important distinction—"minister for" means that they are waiting for our instructions. We need to speak to activate them. They are waiting to respond to our words; they will not automatically look into every need that we have.

You activate angels when you declare, "Surely He shall deliver you from the snare of the fowler and from the perilous pestilence." Trigger your heavenly army when you proclaim, "A thousand may fall at your side, and ten thousand at your right hand; but it shall not come near you." Our Lord Jesus Himself demonstrated the importance of speaking aloud God's Word in the wilderness when three times He said, "It is written" and quoted God's Word. I don't know about you, but I intend to speak forth God's Word!

Today's Prayer
Heavenly Father, thank You that Your angels heed the
voice of Your Word and are sent forth to minister for me.
Thank You that as I speak forth Your Word, Your angels
are activated to help me. Thank You for revealing to me
the power of Your Word. Help me to get Your promises
on the inside of me and to speak your Word
over my circumstances. Amen.

Today's Thought
Every time I quote the Scriptures out loud and give voice to
God's Word, I activate His angels to minister for me.

MAY YOUR EYES BE OPENED

The eyes of your understanding being enlightened;
that you may know what is the hope of His calling,
what are the riches of the glory of His inheritance
in the saints, and what is the exceeding greatness
of His power toward us who believe.

—*Ephesians 1:18–19*

I have another testimony from a key pastor in our church. He and his wife were planning for a short vacation in Hong Kong to celebrate their wedding anniversary. They had set their eyes on a particular hotel in the city. However, no matter how hard they tried, they were unable to secure a room. Frustrated and disappointed, they had no choice but to change their plans.

Sometime later, that hotel was all over the newspapers. It turned out that in the very same week that they had originally planned to stay there, there was an outbreak of a deathly disease. Someone who was staying at the hotel had died of a highly contagious virus, triggering a lockdown. All hotel guests had to be quarantined and some were found to have contracted the virus as well.

What had initially been a disappointment for this couple turned out to be God's hand of protection upon them. Who is to say that angels weren't working overtime on their behalf to thwart their travel plans and prevent them from being at the wrong place at the wrong time? After all, Psalm 91 promises that no plague would come near their dwelling.

My friend, I pray, according to today's Scripture, that the eyes of your understanding may be enlightened, that you may know the riches of the glory of His inheritance in the saints, and what is the exceeding greatness of His power toward us who believe. I pray that like Elisha, you will be able to see beyond that which is in the natural realm, and see the legions of angels that are poised to minister for you. The Bible tells us that "the things which are seen *are* temporary, but the things which *are* not seen are eternal" (2 Cor. 4:18).

Today, we might not physically see angels, but we know they are here with us. The Lord has promised that He will never leave us nor forsake us (see Heb. 13:5). He has promised that His goodness and mercy will follow us all the days of our lives (see Ps. 23:6). Our confidence is not in what we see but in His promises that are everlasting, and as you put your trust in the Lord, I pray that you will experience every blessing that the Lord Jesus has purchased for you on the cross of Calvary!

Today's Prayer

Father God, I ask You to enlighten the eyes of
my understanding to see beyond the natural realm,
and see the legions of angles that are poised to minister
for me. Thank You for the exceeding greatness of Your
grace and Your power toward me. I declare that as I put
my trust in You, Your angels are with me to ensure
no evil befalls me. Amen.

Today's Thought

I may not physically see angels, but I know in my heart that
legions of angels are here with me to help me.

TIME TO PLAY OFFENSE

You shall tread upon the lion and the cobra,
The young lion and the serpent you
shall trample underfoot.

—Psalm 91:13

AUTHORITY OVER THE ENEMY

You shall tread upon the lion and the cobra, the young lion and the serpent you shall trample underfoot.

—*Psalm 91:13*

✥

Do you know that as a believer in Christ, you have authority over the enemy?

It is true that the devil is the god of this fallen world (see 2 Cor. 4:4 NASB), who "walks about like a roaring lion, seeking whom he may devour" (1 Pet. 5:8). But we, as believers, are not called to cower in fear like the people of the world, for God's eternal Word proclaims that "He who is in you is greater than he who is in the world" (1 John 4:4).

In Christ, we have authority over the devil and all his cohorts. In Christ, we have authority to *tread upon the lion and the cobra*. The fowler's snares shall be foiled and the hunter shall be the hunted. Our role in this increasingly dangerous world isn't to be passive and indifferent, waiting to be devoured by the roaring lion. We are endued with power and authority to hunt down the roaring lion!

The Bible records the account of how Samson was in the vineyards of Timnah when suddenly "a young lion *came* roaring against him" (Judg. 14:5). Now, what would you do if *you* were suddenly ambushed by a lion?

Psychologists tell us that there are essentially three possible responses that are instinctively triggered when a person is unexpectedly thrust into an extremely dangerous situation—fight, take flight, or freeze. While most of us would probably either take flight or freeze, Samson instinctively rose to fight: "the Spirit of the LORD came mightily upon him, and he tore the lion apart as one would have torn apart a young goat, though *he had* nothing in his hand" (Judg. 14:6). Now, *that's* taking authority! The hunter came at Samson but found itself the hunted!

Sometime later, Samson passed by the lion's carcass and saw a swarm of bees and some honey in it. So he scooped out some of the honey and ate it. It was from this experience that Samson came up with this riddle, "Out of the eater came something to eat, and out of the strong came something sweet" (Judg. 14:14).

There is a beautiful picture here for all of us. Instead of being eaten by the lion, Samson obtained something sweet to eat. What is the spiritual truth for us today? Out of every evil and negative thing the devil throws at you today, God will make something sweet for you. Your giants will be as bread to you. God will turn every bitter adversity into sweet honey for you!

Today's Prayer

Lord Jesus, thank You for Your mighty presence in my life. Thank You for giving me the power and authority to trample upon the devil and all his cohorts. I believe that You will turn every evil and negative situation the devil throws at me into something sweet for me. I declare that my giants will be as bread to me because You are with me and for me. Amen.

Today's Thought

In Christ, I have been endued with power and authority over the enemy, and God will turn every evil and negative thing the devil throws at me into something sweet for me.

GET READY TO PLAY OFFENSE

He who is in you is greater than he who is in the world.

—*1 John 4:4*

❧

Whatever team sports you follow, you know that defense is vital. A good defensive strategy keeps you in contention, but defense alone doesn't win championships.

The prayer of protection in Psalm 91 has many defensive elements. We've talked about dwelling in the secret place of the Most High, abiding under the shadow of the Almighty, and taking the Lord as our refuge and fortress. We've seen how we are covered under His wings and protected by an angelic army. Now that we've got our defensive game covered, are you ready to play some offense?

Certainly, there are times and seasons when the best thing to do is to take cover and to allow ourselves to be sheltered. The Lord is our safe house, our hiding place, and our impenetrable fortress, and I love that we get to take refuge in Him. But the prayer of protection also declares this in verse 13 (boldface mine): "You shall **tread upon** the lion and the cobra, the young lion and the serpent you shall **trample underfoot**."

That's taking an offensive position. That's going on the attack. That's taking authority!

In the Gospel of Luke, we see our Lord Jesus sending seventy disciples out against the kingdom of darkness, as "lambs among wolves" (Luke 10:3). Have you ever *seen* a lamb overpower a wolf? Of course not. You see, this authority that we are talking about is not natural authority. Like the lamb, you and I have no power in and of ourselves. This is a supernatural authority that comes from our Lord Jesus Christ, just as the strength that enabled Samson to tear apart the young lion was a supernatural strength.

The portrayals of Samson I have seen depict a massive and muscular man. I think he could have been small and scrawny, but endued with supernatural power and might from God. Naturally speaking, for Samson to take on the lion with his bare hands was like a lamb taking on a ferocious wolf. But we know that He who is in us is greater than any predator that is in the world. Amen!

My friend, in Christ, you are far stronger than you think you are. You may not look it or feel it, but God always uses the weak things of this world to confound the wise and mighty (see 1 Cor. 1:27). Remember, the race is not always to the swift, nor the battle to the strong. It is *the Lord* who ultimately determines who shall emerge victorious. And since the Lord is for you, who can be against you (see Rom. 8:31)!

Today's Prayer
Father in heaven, thank You for Your promise that I will tread upon and trample the enemy underfoot. Thank You that in Christ Jesus, You have endued me with supernatural power and might to not be afraid of the enemy and to have victory over him. I declare that greater is He who is in me than the enemy who is in the world. Amen.

Today's Thought
I have no power in and of myself, but I have supernatural authority and power through the Lord Jesus Christ to trample the enemy underfoot.

THE ENEMY IS BENEATH YOUR FEET

Then the seventy returned with joy, saying, "Lord, even
the demons are subject to us in Your name." And He said
to them, "I saw Satan fall like lightning from heaven.
*Behold, **I give you the authority to trample on serpents***
and scorpions, and over all the power of the enemy,
and nothing shall by any means hurt you."
—Luke 10:17–19 *(boldface mine)*

In the previous reading, we saw our Lord Jesus sending seventy disciples out against the kingdom of darkness, as "lambs among wolves." Look in today's Scripture at the exchange between the seventy disciples and the Lord Jesus when they returned. My friend, the power and authority our Lord Jesus gave them to operate in is the power and authority we have as believers today!

Romans 16:20 declares that the God of peace will crush Satan underneath our feet! He is a defeated foe. The Bible is very consistent and always puts the devil *beneath your feet* (see Gen. 3:15, Eph. 1:22). You are not at the mercy of the enemy's attacks. Don't put him on a pedestal, as if he has power and dominion over you. Remind yourself that in Christ, you are "far above all principality and power and might and dominion" (Eph. 1:21), and every lion and serpent you shall trample underfoot!

We exercise our authority as believers when we go on the offensive against the enemy today. How do we do that? We wield the sword of the Spirit, which is the Word of God! Our authority, our strength, and our victory are found in His Word.

Look at how the Bible describes the armor of God: "Stand therefore, having girded your waist with truth, having put on the breastplate of righteousness, and having shod your feet with the preparation of the gospel of peace; above all, taking the shield of faith with which you will be able to quench all the fiery darts of the wicked one. And take the helmet of salvation, and the sword of the Spirit, which is the word of God" (Eph. 6:14–17).

Do you see that the sword of the Spirit, which is the Word of God, is the only piece of the armor that is offensive? That is why, for every round of attack the devil launched at our Lord Jesus, He fought back with the sword of the Spirit—He used the written Word of God.

When we pray the prayer of protection in Psalm 91, we are praying according to the Word of God and wielding the sword of the Spirit. So no matter what report is roaring at you, be it from doctors, bankers, or from the news media, take your place of authority and lay hold of Scriptures for your situation. Fight back with the Word of God!

_____

Today's Prayer

Father God, thank You that the devil is beneath my feet because I am in Christ. Thank You that You have given me authority over all the power of the enemy and nothing shall by any means hurt me. Thank You for Your Word, the sword of the Spirit, with which I can counter every attack of the enemy and experience victory. Amen.

Today's Thought

I have authority over all the power of the enemy and I have the sword of the Spirit to go on the offensive against every attack.

TAKE AUTHORITY OVER YOUR SITUATION

*Then Peter said, "Silver and gold I do not have,
but what I do have I give you: In the name of
Jesus Christ of Nazareth, rise up and walk."*

—*Acts 3:6*

❦

In the previous reading, we saw how you can take authority over your situation by standing on the Word of God. Join
me in reading this wonderful report that Gisele from Texas
shared with me that demonstrates how this works:

*My husband had surgery for hiatal hernia. It was a sim-
ple procedure where a piece of mesh was inserted into
the affected area and he was able to return home the
same day. However, he became increasingly unwell after
he got home. He was feeling very bloated, had a lot of
pain, and was running a fever. He was admitted back to
the hospital and we spent the next week there.*

*It turned out that a bowel obstruction was caus-
ing all his problems. Another surgery was planned.
Honestly, we felt very discouraged and defeated at that*

point. Then, I remembered learning a few weeks earlier from Joseph Prince about how Christians should take charge and command symptoms to go using the Word of God. I told my husband about it and we prayed, speaking God's Word. I also commanded the bowel obstruction to be gone in Jesus' name.

Later that night, my husband went for a series of abdominal tests. These were tests that the hospital had been conducting twice daily since his admission to benchmark his progress. The next morning, when the tests were being done again, my husband started feeling great and announced that he was going home.

The doctor was thrilled with his huge turnaround and told us that the blockage, which had been detected in all the other tests done previously, was not found in the last two tests. So my husband was discharged and we went home. Praise the Lord for His protection and healing!

All glory to our Lord Jesus Christ. I love how Gisele did not take flight or freeze when she came under attack, even though as a couple they felt discouraged when they heard the doctor's report. She quickly put into practice what she'd heard me teach about exercising our authority through using the Word. She and her husband prayed, speaking God's Word over his body, *and* she commanded the negative symptoms to go in Jesus' name, as the apostle Peter did in today's Scripture from the book of Acts.

That, my friend, is how we go on the offensive against the enemy today.

Today's Prayer

Heavenly Father, thank You that no matter what negative report is roaring at me, I can pray according to Your Word and wield the sword of the Spirit to see victory. Thank You that I can always take my place of authority in Christ by declaring Your Word of healing and protection over my life and my family's. Amen.

Today's Thought

No matter what negative report is roaring at me, I take my place of authority in Christ and choose to speak forth God's Word to experience victory.

THE ROARING LION

Be sober, be vigilant; because your adversary
the devil walks about like a roaring lion,
seeking whom he may devour.

—1 Peter 5:8

❧

Isn't it interesting in the above passage that the devil has to *seek out* those whom he *may* devour? This means that he can't devour everyone. Don't surrender your authority to him and be found among those whom he can devour! Also, did you notice that he roams about *like*, or *as*, "a roaring lion"? I asked the Lord why the devil goes about as a roaring lion and not some other creature. He led me to Proverbs 19:12, which says, "The king's wrath *is* like **the roaring of a lion**" (boldface mine). The devil is an imposter who goes about as a roaring lion because he is imitating the King of kings, our Lord Jesus, the real lion of Judah. He wants people to think that our King is full of wrath, anger, and rage against us. He comes at us roaring with the voice of condemnation, accusation, and shame.

Satan wants you to have the impression that you have

failed God, and that He is not only disappointed with you, but is also downright furious with you. Now, if you believe that about God, would you be taking refuge under the shelter of His wings? Would you be taking your rightful place of authority, power, and strength? Of course not. In fact, you will flee from God!

Believers who are under a cloud of condemnation won't pray the prayer of protection. They feel unworthy of God's promises and, in fact, are expecting punishment and judgment from God. That is exactly where the devil wants you to be. When you run away from God, you are running straight into the devil's snare. You abdicate your place of authority when you abdicate your place of intimacy with God.

Beloved, you need to know this: You are loved. God is not mad at you. In Christ, you can have the confident assurance that you are forgiven, loved, and righteous (see Eph. 1:7, Rom. 8:37, 2 Cor. 5:21). The Lord Jesus has taken all your punishment at the cross so that today, you can enjoy His undeserved, unearned, and unmerited favor. God sees you *in Christ*, who is completely spotless and without blame.

Based on our own deeds, none of us qualify for His protection. But because of what our Lord Jesus has done for us on the cross, we can all come boldly to His throne of grace (see Heb. 4:16). Because of what He has done, we qualify to dwell in the secret place with the King of kings, where the phony "roaring lion" has no power over us!

Today's Prayer

Beloved Lord Jesus, thank You for taking all my punishment on the cross so that today, the Father sees me completely spotless and without blame in You. Thank You for bringing me into an intimate relationship with You, where I can rest in Your love and protection. As I dwell in the secret place with You, I declare that the phony "roaring lion" has no power over me. Amen.

Today's Thought

God sees me in Christ, who is completely spotless and without blame. Because of what the Lord Jesus has done for me on the cross, I can access the secret place where the phony "roaring lion" has no power over me.

BOLD AS A LION

The king's wrath is like the roaring of a lion,
*but **his favor** is **like dew on the grass**.*

—*Proverbs 19:12 (boldface mine)*

∽∧∾

Continuing with our teaching on the roaring lion in Proverbs 19:12, I want you to see the verse in its entirety. Today, we are beneficiaries of God's favor, because His wrath against our sins has already been completely satisfied at Calvary. In Hebrew, the word used for "favor" is *ratsown*, which means His pleasure, delight, goodwill, and acceptance.[22]

Our place of protection was purchased with the blood of our Lord Jesus Christ. In Him, we have been made righteous, and all the blessings of the righteous, including protection, provision, and length of days, are our inheritance. That's the place we are in today. Isn't that beautiful? No wonder the Scriptures tell us, "The wicked flee when no one pursues, but the righteous are bold as a lion" (Prov. 28:1). It also tells us, "The effective, fervent prayer of a righteous man avails much" (James 5:16). A righteous man (or woman) is who you are in Christ, and when you pray the prayer of protection in Psalm 91, your prayers avail much, for God answers your prayers!

I received a testimony of God's divine protection from Sally, who lives in South Africa. Be encouraged as you read how she prayed for protection knowing that she is righteous in Christ:

> *I was driving a rented car when I heard a loud bang. Within moments, the car was on fire. I immediately switched off the engine to get out. But to my horror, I could not remove the seat belt or open the door! I was stuck.*
>
> *Finally, I managed to get the door opened. By then, the flames were threatening to come inside the car and I had to close the door again because I was trapped by the seat belt. I called out to Abba Father and just declared, "I am Your righteousness. You are the only One who can save me!" As those words were echoing in my ears and heart, I heard a click as the seat belt was released. I dashed out of the car.*
>
> *When the fire department arrived, they were able to stop the blaze. I praise the Lord for delivering me safely out of this dangerous situation! I realized that the devil has long been defeated and we don't have to fear anything anymore.*

Praise the Lord for His deliverance and protection. I

rejoice that we are shielded from danger because of the righteousness we have in Christ!

Today's Prayer

Abba, Father, thank You that Your favor covers me like dew on the grass. Thank You that I have been made righteous in Your Son, and all the blessings of the righteous, including protection, provision, and length of days, are mine. I can boldly face life and be bold in my prayers because I know You hear me and will answer. Amen.

Today's Thought

In Christ, I have been made righteous, and all the blessings of the righteous, including protection, provision, and length of days, are my inheritance. I can face life with boldness and be bold in my prayers.

IS THERE NO SUFFERING FOR THE BELIEVER?

For to you it has been granted on behalf
of Christ, not only to believe in Him,
but also to suffer for His sake.

—Philippians 1:29

Am I saying that there's no suffering in the body of Christ? My dear reader, none of these protection truths shared from God's Word negates the fact that we are called and given the privilege to suffer persecution for His name's sake as the apostle Paul states in today's Scripture. Furthermore, Paul tells his protégé, Timothy, "Everyone who wants to live a godly life in Christ Jesus will suffer persecution" (2 Tim. 3:12 NLT). Jesus Himself said that those who follow Him will be persecuted for His name's sake (see Matt. 10:22). Be clear that this persecution doesn't involve terminal illnesses, tragic accidents, or premature death.

But Pastor Prince, wasn't Job a righteous man who experienced terrible suffering?

I have preached a full message on Job and it is not the focus of this book to cover the full spectrum of Job's suffering. However, you can get the full audio message here: JosephPrince. com/whataboutjob. For now, I want you to see that what happened to Job is not something that will happen to you who are IN CHRIST today. You see, one of Job's complaints was this: "If only there were a mediator between us, someone who could bring us together" (Job 9:33 NLT). Now, read these powerful words spoken by Elihu in Job 33:23–24, which describes this mediator: "If there is a messenger for him, a mediator, one among a thousand, to show man His uprightness, then He is gracious to him, and says, 'Deliver him from going down to the Pit; I have found a ransom.'"

Elihu's description of a mediator foreshadows what 1 Timothy 2:5–6 tells us, "For *there is* one God and one Mediator between God and men, *the* Man Christ Jesus, who gave Himself a ransom for all, to be testified in due time." Job experienced his sufferings because he didn't have a mediator. But today, you and I do—in the person of our Lord Jesus, who died at the cross to atone for our sins and made us righteous before God. He became our ransom (the Hebrew word for ransom comes from the root word *kaphar*, which means "to make an atonement"[23]).

Beloved, the atoning blood of Christ has canceled all the legal rights that the enemy had against you and your family.

When you receive all that His perfect sacrifice at the cross has accomplished for you, you don't have to live afraid that you will be like Job. Unlike Job, you have a mediator—Christ Jesus. In Him you can look forward to a future full of His promises, blessings, and protection (see Ps. 23:6)!

Today's Prayer
Father, thank You for the atoning blood of Christ that has canceled all the legal rights that the enemy had against me and my family. I choose to receive all that His perfect sacrifice has accomplished for me, and I look forward to a future full of Your promises, blessings, and protection. Amen.

Today's Thought
I have no reason to fear because the atoning blood of Christ has canceled all the legal rights that the enemy had against me and my family.

AUTHORITY OVER DEATH

For I am already being poured out as a drink offering,
and the time of my departure is at hand. ***I have***
fought the good fight, I have finished the race,
I have kept the faith. Finally, there is laid up for
me the crown of righteousness.

—2 Timothy 4:6–8 (boldface mine)

At this point, you may be wondering, *If as believers we have*
authority over the enemy, why were the apostle Paul and some
of the other apostles martyred? Didn't they have the authority to
crush the enemies who were after their lives?

First, let me submit to you that they *chose* to be martyred—it was not something that caught them by surprise. Let me show you some evidence of this from the Word of God.

Hebrews chapter 11 recounts the amazing heroes of faith down through the corridors of time, those "who through faith subdued kingdoms, worked righteousness, obtained promises, stopped the mouths of lions, quenched the violence of fire, escaped the edge of the sword, out of weakness were made strong, became valiant in battle, turned to flight the armies of the aliens. Women received their dead raised to life again. Others were tortured, **not accepting deliverance**" (Heb. 11:33–35, boldface mine). The phrase "not accepting deliverance" tells us that they *were offered* deliverance, but they *chose not to accept it*. This was because they chose to be with Jesus "that they might obtain a better resurrection."

Listen to how the apostle Paul spoke about his life: "For to me, living means living for Christ, and **dying is even better**. But if I live, I can do more fruitful work for Christ. So I really don't know which is better. I'm torn between two desires: I long to go and **be with Christ, which would be far better for me**. But for your sakes, it is better that I continue to live. Knowing this, I am convinced that I will remain alive so I can continue to help all of you grow and experience the joy of your faith" (Phil. 1:21–25 NLT, boldface mine).

Hey, these are the words of a man who had power over life and death! It's far from some erroneous teachings I've heard from people, who tell you that "when your time comes," you will die and you have no say in the matter. I don't know what their Bibles say, but my Bible says, "With long life I will *satisfy you*" (see Ps. 91:16). All of us have a free choice to use our faith to believe God for a long life. How long a life? That depends on you—according to your faith and satisfaction be it unto you.

As for the apostle Paul, we know that he *was* satisfied before he was martyred because in the last chapter of his last epistle, he penned his epilogue in today's Scripture from 2 Timothy 4. He decided that he had fought a good fight and had finished the race. It was enough; he was satisfied. We see here a man with authority over death. Paul was not murdered; he was ready to go.

Now, there were instances earlier in Paul's life when Paul was not yet ready to go. Once, when he was stoned, dragged out of the city of Lystra, and left for dead, he got back up, went back into the city, and continued preaching the gospel of grace (see Acts 14:19–21). Death had no hold on him! On another occasion, when he was on the island of Malta, a poisonous snake bit him but he merely shook it off into the fire (see Acts 28:3–6 NLT). The serpent had no power over the apostle Paul.

Dear reader, the same authority over the enemy that the apostle Paul had belongs to you and me today. Whatever the roaring lion or poisonous serpent is attacking you with today, remember, its rightful place is underneath your feet. Hallelujah!

Today's Prayer

Father in heaven, I choose to use my faith to believe
You for a long life that is full of good days. I declare
that the attacks of the enemy cannot prevail against me
for I am Yours and my life has been purchased with
Jesus' precious blood. Thank You for giving
me a long, satisfying life. Amen.

Today's Thought

Death cannot dictate to me when my time is up,
because I choose to believe God for a long,
satisfying life that is full of good days.

PROTECTED BY THE FATHER'S LOVE

*"Because he has set his love upon Me,
therefore I will deliver him;
I will set him on high,
because he has known My name."*

—*Psalm 91:14*

GOD SO LOVED US

"Because he has set his love upon Me, therefore
I will deliver him; I will set him on high,
because he has known My name."

—*Psalm 91:14*

❧

What qualifies you for God's protection? I ask this question because I have heard many ministers whose teachings make it seem like you have to *qualify* for God's blessings. They make it sound like God blesses you *only* if you are able to love the Lord with all your heart, with all your soul, and with all your mind. This also applies in the area of your protection. When they read, "**Because** he has set his love upon Me, **therefore** I will deliver him" (boldface mine), they conclude that God's protection is dependent on us fulfilling the condition of loving the Lord perfectly.

Unfortunately, such teaching robs you of the faith to believe God for divine protection over yourself and your loved ones. Anything that is dependent on *our* efforts is on a shaky foundation, because no matter how "good" a Christian we think we are, our love for the Lord *will* fail. That is precisely why God sent His Son. He knew that man would never be able to fulfill all His commandments. In sending His Son, He was saying to us, "I know you can't, so let *Me* love you with all My heart, all My mind, and all My strength." Therein lies the beautiful love story we call the gospel of Jesus Christ.

God SO loved the world that He sent His only begotten Son to save and ransom us. The Lord Jesus Christ Himself fulfilled *all* the requirements of the law. Today, even when our love for Him wavers, even when we fail, He still delivers us from evil!

One Scripture that beautifully encapsulates the crux of the new covenant of grace is 1 John 4:10 (boldface mine): "In this is love, **not that we loved God, but that He loved us** and sent His Son *to be* the propitiation [the atoning sacrifice] for our sins." I pray that your heart will be anchored on this revelation. The emphasis of the new covenant is God's love for you, not your love for God.

Am I saying that your love for God is unimportant? Of course not. What I am saying is that our love for Him will always waver, but His love *never* fails. The Bible declares that "the steadfast love of the Lord **never ceases**" (Lam. 3:22 ESV, boldface mine). I am so grateful that we are under the new covenant of God's amazing grace, where we can depend on *His* unconditional, unchanging, and irrevocable love for us!

Today's Prayer

*Abba, Father, thank You that You so loved me that
You sent Your only begotten Son to save and ransom me.
Thank You that Your love for me never wavers and never
fails, even when my love for You is not perfect and fails.
I am so grateful for Your amazing grace that alone
qualifies me for Your protection. Amen.*

Today's Thought

*It is the steadfast, unwavering love of God for me—
not my imperfect love for Him—that qualifies me
for His protection.*

THE CROSS HAS MADE A DIFFERENCE

For He made Him who knew no sin to be sin for us, that we might become the righteousness of God in Him.
—*2 Corinthians 5:21*

Under the old covenant, it is true that God's protection *was* conditional. But for you and me today, it is vital that we read and understand Psalm 91 through the lens of the new covenant—through the lens of the cross. We are no longer living under the old covenant. We have a new and living way (see Heb. 10:20)! Under the old, protection is *achieved*. Under the new, protection is *received*. I have covered the differences between law and grace extensively in my other books such as *Destined To Reign* and *Grace Revolution*, so I won't delve too deeply into this subject here. All I really want you to see is this: *The cross has made a difference.*

At the cross, God "made Him who knew no sin *to be* sin for us, that we might become the righteousness of God in Him" (2 Cor. 5:21). Today, we *are* the righteousness of God in Christ! Because we are righteous in Christ, we can receive the promise of Psalm 5:12, which declares, "For You, O LORD, will bless the righteous; with favor You will surround him as *with* a shield." Naturally, we can't always watch our backs. But supernaturally, God has got us covered all around. His abundant supply of grace (unmerited favor) encompasses us like a mighty and impenetrable force field, surrounding us 360 degrees and twenty-four hours a day!

Coming back to Psalm 91:14, how do we set our love upon God today? We set our love upon God by meditating on, talking about, and listening to preaching about His love for us! Remember, it is not about our love for Him, but His love for us. It is about us meditating on Bible verses such as, "For God so greatly loved *and* dearly prized the world that He [even] gave up His only begotten (unique) Son, so that whoever believes in (trusts in, clings to, relies on) Him shall not perish (come to destruction, be lost) but have eternal (everlasting) life" (John 3:16 AMPC).

There is protection and deliverance from destruction when you believe in God's love for you. Set your mind on how greatly loved and dearly prized you are. The more conscious you are of the Lord's love for you, the more His protection will manifest in your life!

Today's Prayer

Lord Jesus, thank You that in You I am the righteousness of God. Thank You that because I am righteous, God's abundant supply of grace (unmerited favor) encompasses me like a mighty and impenetrable force field all around. I choose to be conscious of, and meditate on, Your love for me today. Amen.

Today's Thought

God's abundant supply of grace (unmerited favor) encompasses me like a mighty and impenetrable force field, surrounding me 360 degrees and twenty-four hours a day!

THE GOD WHO SHUTS THE LIONS' MOUTHS

Not a scratch was found on him, for he had trusted in his God.

—Daniel 6:23 NLT

Daniel in the Old Testament is a good example of a man who set his mind on the Lord's love for him and experienced the Lord's deliverance. The Word of God tells us that Daniel had such great favor with King Darius that the other officials did all they could to dig up some dirt on him. But try as they might, they found him to be "faithful, always responsible, and completely trustworthy" (Dan. 6:4 NLT). The only snare they could devise was to point to Daniel's devotion to his God. (What a glorious accusation!)

They observed that without fail, Daniel would go to his upper room three times a day, get on his knees, and, with his windows open toward Jerusalem, pray and give thanks to his God. These officials then tricked the king into signing a law decreeing that for thirty days, no one was to pray to anyone, divine or human, except to King Darius. If this decree was violated, the offender was to be thrown into a den of lions. They knew with certainty that Daniel would not stop praying to his God. Sure enough, even after Daniel had heard about the new decree, he went up to his room and prayed to God just as he had always done.

The officials, who had gone to Daniel's house to catch him praying to God, went straight to King Darius. They reminded him of the law that he had signed and with mock chagrin accused Daniel of defying the king and his law. When the king heard their accusation, the Bible tells us that he was "greatly displeased," not with Daniel, but with himself because of his love for Daniel. For the rest of the day, he tried to find a way to save Daniel (see Dan. 6:14).

However, once an official law of the Medes and the Persians was issued, it could not be revoked. The king's hand was forced—he had no choice but to give the order for Daniel to be cast into the den of lions. The worried king spent the night fasting and refused his usual entertainment. Tossing and turning in his bed, he could not sleep at all. Very early the next morning, the king rushed to the lions' den. The Bible tells us, "When he got there, he called out in anguish, 'Daniel, servant of the living God! Was your God, whom you serve so faithfully, able to rescue you from the lions?' Daniel answered, 'Long live the king! My God sent his angel to shut the lions' mouths so that they would not hurt me, for I have been found innocent in his sight. And I have not wronged you, Your Majesty.' The king was overjoyed and ordered that Daniel be lifted from the den. **Not a scratch was found on him, for he had trusted in his God**" (Dan. 6:20–23 NLT, boldface mine).

Now that you are more acquainted with Psalm 91, I am sure you can see many elements of the psalm in this account of God's deliverance. Daniel was clearly a man who dwelt daily in the secret place of the Most High, under the shadow of His wings. Daniel set his heart toward the Lord, praying and giving thanks to God three times a day. We also see God's angels in action and Daniel taking authority over fearsome, hungry lions within mere feet of him! In fact, he did not even suffer a single scratch after being shut up in a den full of lions for a whole night.

In contrast, when King Darius later ordered the officials who had schemed against Daniel to be thrown into the den, the lions "leaped on them and tore them apart before they even hit the floor of the den" (Dan. 6:24 NLT). Truly, the Lord was Daniel's refuge and fortress—as He is yours today.

Today's Prayer

*Father God, thank You for showing me through the
story of Daniel what a loving and faithful God You are. I
thank You that as I set my mind on how greatly loved
I am by You, You will protect and deliver me no matter
how ferocious the threat, such that I walk free
without even so much as a scratch. Amen.*

Today's Thought

*As I set my mind on how greatly loved I am by God,
He will protect and deliver me no matter
how ferocious the threat.*

SEEK THE PROTECTOR

When You said, "Seek My face," my heart said to You,
"Your face, Lord, I will seek."

—*Psalm 27:8*

In the previous reading, we saw that Daniel made a habit of praying three times a day. Now, depending on how established you are in God's grace, you can interpret that as a religious routine, or you can see his dedicated prayer time as an outward expression of his intimate relationship with the Lord. Please be clear about this. I am not saying that if we want to be protected like Daniel, we have to pray three times a day. What I have really been saying throughout this book is that protection is *a result of closeness and intimacy* with the Lord.

There are no formulas, steps, or shortcuts to walking in divine protection. Simply walk close with the Lord and you will unconsciously be under the shadow of His wings. Don't just pursue the protection, seek the Protector! You can recite Psalm 91 fifty times a day, but if you have no relationship with Jesus, there will be no results. The prayer of protection is not transactional; it is *relational*.

You've missed the point if you have to ask how many times a day you should pray. That is equivalent to asking your spouse, "How many times a day must I kiss you?" I wouldn't want my wife, Wendy, to ask me that! Relationships are birthed from the heart. They are not governed by formulas, rules, or algorithms. You kiss your spouse because of love. It is not an obligation; it is a privilege and pleasure. In the same way, don't mechanize your relationship with God. Every day, you can choose whether or not to meditate on His love for you. Daniel chose to do it three times a day. We can learn from that without turning it into a dry formula.

What Daniel had was an intimate *relationship* with the Lord. I pray that you will have this too. The Bible tells us that in his daily prayers, Daniel was always giving thanks to God. It is so good to live with thanksgiving in your heart toward the Lord. Each and every day, there are so many things that our Lord protects us from that we are not even aware of. Give thanks to Him for His love for you. Praise Him and set your mind daily toward Him. Be so conscious of how close you are to Him and how utterly loved you are—and enjoy the protection that comes from being found in the shadow of His wings!

Today's Prayer

Lord Jesus, thank You that You want me to draw close to You and know You intimately. I thank You that as I just meditate on and enjoy Your love for me, You keep me safe under the shadow of Your wings. I choose to set my heart on You and to seek You above everything else. Amen.

Today's Thought

There are no formulas, steps, or shortcuts to walking in divine protection. Protection is a result of closeness and intimacy with the Lord.

DAY 5

PROTECTION IN THE FATHER

For Christ also suffered once for sins, the just for the unjust, that He might bring us to God, being put to death in the flesh but made alive by the Spirit.

—1 Peter 3:18

Can I show you a beautiful picture of God's love for you found in the story of Daniel? We saw how in Daniel's case, the law of the land was violated and how, in spite of his love for Daniel, the king had to carry out the law and punish Daniel. If he hadn't, he would have been an unrighteous king. Now, imagine if someone came again a year later to accuse Daniel of this crime and asked for Daniel to be punished again, what would the king do? Would the king throw Daniel into the lions' den again? No! Daniel had already been sentenced; he had already paid the price for his violation of the law.

My dear friend, because our Lord Jesus has been punished on the cross in your place, the devil cannot come to the King and ask for you to be punished and thrown into the lions' den. You see, your sins were forgiven not because the King simply decided to close an eye and let you off the hook. The King forgave your sins *righteously* after judging them in the body of our Lord Jesus Christ. He who was completely without sin took your place and bore the full weight of the punishment for your sins (see 2 Cor. 5:21). ALL your sins have been legally and judicially judged at the cross. Because of His finished work, once you received the Lord Jesus into your heart, God's justice and righteousness are on your side!

Do you know how much God loves Jesus, His beloved Son and the apple of His eye? Then I pray that you will have a revelation of how much your Father in heaven loves YOU. To redeem you, God paid the price with the blood of His only Son. It must have been a most difficult decision for Him. None of us would ever fully comprehend what God experienced in sending His own beloved Son to the cross. We catch just a small glimpse of the torment that God suffered when we read about King Darius's suffering. King Darius wanted to save Daniel, but he could not violate his own law. Similarly, God loves His Son, but He knew the only way to save us, who had violated the law, was to sacrifice His own Son, Jesus Christ. May this revelation of His amazing love and grace give you boldness to come freely to Him and find protection under His wings.

Today's Prayer

Father God, thank You that all my sins have been legally and judicially judged on Jesus' body at the cross. Thank You that through faith in Your Son, my sins are righteously forgiven—once for all time. I declare that Your justice and righteousness are on my side today, protecting me and providing for me. Amen.

Today's Thought

Because all my sins have been legally and judicially judged at the cross, God's justice and righteousness are on my side today.

KNOWING HIS NAME

*"I will protect those who trust in **my name**."*

—Psalm 91:14 NLT (boldface mine)

❧

We have talked about seeing the names of God in just the first two verses of Psalm 91 alone, and how that brings revelation and comfort to us. Yet, did you know that Jesus came to reveal only one name?

Our Lord Jesus came to reveal the name "Father." *Father* speaks of family and of closeness and intimacy. You can know God as *Elyon*, the Most High. As *El Shaddai*, God Almighty. As *Yehovah*, the Lord, the covenant-keeping God. As *Elohim*, mighty Creator of the heavens and the earth. Every name is so significant as each one reveals a wonderful aspect of our God. But when you know God as *Father*, *all* His virtues, attributes, and power work *for* you to set you on high and deliver you.

Our Lord Jesus prayed, "Now I am no longer in the world, but these are in the world, and I come to You. Holy Father, keep through Your name those whom You have given Me, that they may be one as We *are*" (John 17:11). The Greek word for "keep" here is the word *tereo*, which means to attend to carefully, to take care of, to guard, to watch, and to preserve.[24] What is the name through which you will be kept guarded and protected? FATHER. Beloved, I want you to know beyond the shadow of a doubt that you have a heavenly Father who loves you, who gave up His all for you, and who is vigilantly watching over you!

He is your Father. Your Daddy. Your Abba.

That is the name by which He wants you to call Him. When my son, Justin, has a nightmare, he doesn't call out, "Pastor Prince!" He just cries out, "Abba!" and I am there, ready to take on any monsters hiding under his bed. In the same way, you can have complete assurance that when you call upon your Father, He *will* answer you. You can have full confidence in your Father's protection and deliverance for you and your family, not because of your love for Him, but because of *His* love for you.

Today's Prayer

Daddy God, thank You that the Lord Jesus revealed You as our "Father." Thank You that I can call out to You as my Abba, knowing that You love me and gave up Your all for me. I believe and declare that I have Your protection over me and my family because of Your love for me. Amen.

Today's Thought

God is my Father, my Daddy, my Abba, who loves me, who gave His all for me, and who is vigilantly watching over and protecting me and my family.

DAY 7

REST IN THE FATHER'S LOVE

For you did not receive the spirit of bondage again
to fear, but you received the Spirit of adoption
by whom we cry out, "Abba, Father."

—Romans 8:15

Do you want to see how having a revelation of your Father's love for you can keep and preserve you? Let me share with you a glorious testimony from a professional athlete who attends our church in Dallas:

> My wife and I have been attending Grace Revolution Church in Dallas, Texas. It has truly been a year of greater glory in every area of our lives—our marriage, finances, career, and physical bodies. One of the many demonstrations of His amazing love came not long ago.
>
> One Saturday evening, I noticed that my left testicle was enlarged and hard. I knew that something was not right and began to be worried and fearful. But at church the next morning, I felt the Lord encouraging me through Pastor Prince's broadcast message. I was

also prayed over and anointed with oil. When Monday came, my wife and I went to the doctor in a state of peace as we rested in our Father's love.

I was diagnosed with testicular cancer. But despite the doctor's report, we chose to cling to the report of the Lord. We knew our heavenly Father would guide us in the decisions we needed to make and we sensed an overwhelming peace in the midst of the storm. We felt so at rest in the finished work of Jesus and were filled with an unexplainable joy. We believed that just as Jesus is, so was I in my physical body.

The doctor wanted to move forward with surgery to remove the mass in the left testicle. That would be followed up with a computerized tomography (CT) scan to assess what further treatment would be needed. During the consultation, we felt very restful about moving forward with the surgery, believing that I was already healed because of Jesus' finished work. We also continually reminded ourselves of our righteousness in Him as we partook of the Holy Communion daily.

The surgery went very well. However, after the surgery, the doctor spoke to my wife with much concern, as the cancerous mass was very large and belonged to the mixed germ cell tumor category. Despite the doctor's concern, my wife and I continued to believe that I was completely free of cancer in my body.

I went in for another CT scan to see if the cancer had spread to the nearby areas. I went in believing that I was healed and that nothing would be found. When the doctor looked over the report, he was astounded. The CT scan confirmed that I was completely cancer-free and extremely healthy.

The doctor found the report very shocking because his experience had taught him that cancer cells of the size and type that I had would certainly have spread to the surrounding areas. He had already made an appointment for me to see a specialist to discuss the options for chemotherapy and radiation therapy even before the CT scan. However, he agreed that it was no longer necessary!

My wife and I know that our heavenly Father had protected me and kept the cancer contained, and subsequently had it removed. What the enemy tried to use as a setback, our heavenly Father used as a divine set-up. Now, as I share this story with people I cross paths with, I am able to use it as a glorious testimony of the health and wholeness that we have in Jesus. Through the whole experience, my wife and I were able to remain at rest because

we knew that the Father sees us as righteous through His
Son, Jesus, and we are completely loved by Him.

   Glory to God!

Wow. Glory to God indeed! There is such power in knowing that the all-powerful, almighty God of Israel is not someone far away. He paid the price so that you and I could *draw near* to Him.

Today's Prayer

Abba, Father, thank You that I have received the Spirit of
adoption and as Your child I can cry out to You intimately
and know You hear me. Thank You that I can rest in Your
love and protection because of Jesus' finished work on
the cross. I believe that You see me righteous through
the perfect work of Jesus. Amen.

Today's Thought

I can rest in the Father's protection because I know that
I am completely loved by Him and that He sees me
righteous in His Son, Jesus.

IN THE PLACE
OF NEARNESS

Neither death nor life, nor angels nor principalities
nor powers, nor things present nor things to come,
nor height nor depth, nor any other created thing,
shall be able to separate us from the love of God
which is in Christ Jesus our Lord.

—*Romans 8:38–39*

You may have read of how Joseph in the book of Genesis wanted his family to dwell in Goshen, which means "drawing near."²⁵ He wanted them in a place of nearness to him and he told them, "There **I will provide** for you" (Gen. 45:11, bold-face mine).

Beloved, even in the midst of famine, Jesus, our heavenly Joseph, wants us close to Him so He can provide for us. In the book of Exodus, God declared, "I will **set apart the land of Goshen**, in which My people dwell, that no swarms *of flies* shall be there" (Exod. 8:22, boldface mine). In the land of Goshen, God's people were protected from all of the ten plagues that besieged the land of Egypt during the time of

Moses. In the second last of the ten plagues, a thick, paralyzing darkness covered the land of Egypt for three whole days. Yet, during that time, "**all the children of Israel had light in their dwellings**" (Exod. 10:23, boldface mine).

I believe it was a supernatural darkness that covered Egypt, because the Egyptians must have turned to natural resources of light to dispel the darkness—only to find they couldn't. By the same token, it was a supernatural light that the Israelites enjoyed in Goshen, a light the darkness tried to smother but couldn't.

Now, I believe this is prophetic of our times. The Bible is relevant for today. We are living in days where we see darkness—a supernatural darkness—cover the earth. Yet, the Scriptures tell us that even when there's thick and deep darkness all around, the church—you and I, together with our families—can experience and enjoy God's supernatural light in our dwellings. We, who have been drawn near to Him through the work of His Son, can have intimacy with God and enjoy His protective covering to live fear-free and victoriously in these dark times.

Beloved, in the place of nearness, God makes a difference between His people and the people of the world. We are *in* this world, but we are not *of* this world (see John 17:14). We are His. He desires for us to be close to Him so that He can hide us under the shadow of His wings. He paid the price so that we can be called His children. Oh, what manner of love the Father has given unto us, that we should be called the sons and daughters of the Most High (see 1 John 3:1)!

Beloved, whatever may be happening in the world today, you can be bold and fearless because nothing can ever separate you from the love of God, your heavenly Father!

———

Today's Prayer

Abba, Father, thank You that I can draw near to You and enjoy Your supernatural light and covering. Thank You that You paid the price for me to be Your child. I believe that no matter what happens in the world, I can live fear-free and enjoy Your protective covering because nothing can ever separate me from Your love. Amen.

Today's Thought

In the place of nearness to my heavenly Father, where I'm under the shadow of His wings, I can live fear-free and enjoy His protective covering.

WISDOM TO STAY SAFE

"He shall call upon Me, and I will answer him;
I will be with him in trouble;
I will deliver him and honor him."

—*Psalm 91:15*

WHAT A SAVIOR!

*"He shall call upon Me, and I will answer him;
I will be with him in trouble; I will deliver
him and honor him."*

—*Psalm 91:15*

ॐ

We have a God who wants us to run to Him. And the moment we do, He has promised that He *will* answer us. Not "might," or "perhaps," but a definite "will." And He does not stop at merely assuring us that He will answer us. He goes on record for all eternity, saying, "I will be with him in trouble; I **will** deliver him and honor him" (boldface mine).

Do you know why we can have the assurance that when we call on Him, He will answer us? It's because of the divine exchange that took place at the cross, where our Lord Jesus cried out, "My God, My God, why have You forsaken Me?" (Matt. 27:46). He was forsaken—left helpless, totally abandoned, and deserted—so that today, we can have the confidence that our heavenly Father will never leave us nor forsake us (see Heb. 13:5). What a Savior!

Don't you feel so loved and so cherished by our Lord?

And He made it so easy for us to receive His promises—our part is to simply *call upon Him* and let Him be our God. Whatever you may be going through today, call upon Him right now and He will deliver and honor you!

Whenever I am troubled, I tell the Lord, "Lord, I am worried about this situation, but I place it in Your nail-pierced hands right now. I surrender into Your hands all my worries, concerns, and cares in this area." Then, I receive His peace, and when the enemy tries to fire new arrows of fear into my heart and mind, I remind myself that the situation is already in the Lord's hands. I remind myself of His promise that He will deliver me!

Are you living with panic attacks, fear, and chronic anxiety? Don't allow the devil to cripple you with all kinds of negative mental pictures, or by replaying all the worst-case scenarios in your head. Call out to your Savior, Jesus Christ! He wants you to cast "**all** your care upon Him, for **He cares for you**" (1 Pet. 5:7, boldface mine). You are not a sheep without a Shepherd, so stop trying to carry all your cares upon your own shoulders.

Whether it is a physical symptom, a financial challenge, or a family situation that you are anxious about, call upon Him and allow His peace to supernaturally guard your heart in every area that you are troubled (see Phil. 4:6–7).

Today's Prayer

Lord Jesus, thank You that when I call upon You, You will answer and deliver me from whatever is troubling me, as promised in Your Word. Thank You that I can place and leave my troubles and worries in Your nail-pierced hands. I receive Your peace that supernaturally guards my heart and mind in every area that troubles me. Amen.

Today's Thought

Whatever troubles or worries me, I call upon Jesus my Savior and place it in His nail-pierced hands. I will receive and allow His peace to supernaturally guard my heart and mind.

A VERY PRESENT HELP

*God is our refuge and strength, a very present
help in trouble. Therefore we will not fear, even though
the earth be removed, and though the mountains be
carried into the midst of the sea; though its waters
roar and be troubled, though the mountains
shake with its swelling.*

—*Psalm 46:1–3*

❧

What a powerful promise from Psalm 46! We do not need to fear because even in times of turmoil and trouble, God is our very present help, our refuge, and our strength! Our part is to call upon Him and He will answer and deliver us. Melinda, a lady from our church, experienced this for herself and wrote to me to share her testimony:

As I was driving my six-year-old son to school, I exited the freeway and approached a traffic light junction. At that time, we were listening to Pastor Prince's sermon CD in the car and I was amazed by how God had saved Noah and his family from the flood. Suddenly, I heard a loud bang as something hit the back of my car. The next thing I knew, my car was flung into the air. It overturned, landed on its roof, and spun a distance to a halt.

As the car was spinning, I started screaming, "Jesus!" at least five times until the car finally came to a halt. Even though we had spun upside down and my son only had a seat belt strapped across his body, he had been miraculously held to the contour of the seat. His head and legs were not dangling from his seat. His neck could have been broken from the impact of the crash, but he was okay.

My son and I crawled out of the wreck without a scratch or whiplash. We stood by the side of the road and a lot of passersby came to our aid. After we had gotten out of the car wreck, the picture of Jesus bleeding on the cross kept flashing in my mind. I knew that my son and I didn't have to bleed on the road that morning because Jesus had shed His blood for us.

When my husband came to get us, he shared that he had also been driving to work around the time of the car accident, and how he felt prompted by the Holy Spirit to switch off the radio and pray in tongues. He also confessed the Lord's favor over our lives, something that we had learned in church the day before.

Jesus turned a possibly tragic accident into a

victorious outcome. No amount of safe driving could have saved our lives, only Jesus and nothing else!

Praise the Lord! In her time of trouble, Melinda cried out the name of Jesus and He answered her. No matter what situation you are in, the Lord is with you and will surely deliver you when you call upon His name!

Today's Prayer

Father, thank You that You are my very present help, my refuge, and my strength in trouble. Thank You that You are always with me and will deliver me when I call upon Your name. Whatever my circumstances, I will not be afraid for You are my ever-present Savior, my deliverer, and my protector. Amen.

Today's Thought

God is my very present help, my refuge, and my strength in trouble. Therefore, I will not fear nor let my heart be troubled.

JESUS IS WITH US IN OUR TROUBLES

*"Blessed be the God of Shadrach, Meshach, and
Abed-Nego, who sent His Angel and delivered
His servants who trusted in Him."*

—*Daniel 3:28*

The book of Daniel records how King Nebuchadnezzar of Babylon made a towering golden statue and commanded all in his kingdom to bow down before it and worship it. Three young men, Shadrach, Meshach, and Abednego, whom the king had appointed to oversee the province of Babylon, refused to do so. Humiliated by their defiance, the king was livid. He gave them one more chance to bow down and worship his golden statue or be thrown immediately into a blazing furnace.

Without flinching, they said, "O Nebuchadnezzar, we do not need to defend ourselves before you. If we are thrown into the blazing furnace, the God whom we serve is able to save us. He will rescue us from your power, Your Majesty. But even if he doesn't…we will never serve your gods or worship the gold statue you have set up" (Dan. 3:16–18 NLT). The king commanded that the furnace be heated seven times hotter than usual, and ordered some of his strongest soldiers to bind them and throw them into the furnace. The furnace was so hot that the flames killed the soldiers as they threw the three men into the roaring flames, securely bound.

Suddenly, the king jumped up in amazement and exclaimed to his officials, "Did we not cast three men bound into the midst of the fire?" They answered and said to the king, "True, O king." "Look!" he answered, "I see four men loose, walking in the midst of the fire; and they are not hurt, and the form of the fourth is like the Son of God" (Dan. 3:24–25). Nebuchadnezzar called out, "Shadrach, Meshach, and Abednego, servants of the Most High God, come out! Come here!" The three men stepped out of the fire and all the officials and advisers crowded around them and "saw that the fire had not touched them. Not a hair on their heads was singed, and their clothing was not scorched" (Dan. 3:26–27 NLT). In fact, the flames only served to loose them from their bonds.

Amazed at how their God had protected them, Nebuchadnezzar began praising God himself. The king then issued a decree stating that if any person spoke a word against the God of Shadrach, Meshach, and Abednego, they would be cut in pieces and their houses would be turned into ash heaps "because there is no other God who can deliver like this" (Dan. 3:29). Then, the king promoted the three men to even higher positions in the province of Babylon.

Beloved, this is *your* God.

Today's Prayer

Lord Jesus, there is truly no other God who saves and delivers like You. Thank You for showing me I need not fear even when I'm in the blazing furnace, because You are with me and will walk with me in the fire and protect me. I believe that You will turn every bad situation around for my good and for Your glory. Amen.

Today's Thought

Even in the midst of the blazing fire, Jesus is with me to deliver and protect me.

NO SMELL OF SMOKE ON YOU

*So Shadrach, Meshach, and Abednego stepped out
of the fire. Then the high officers, officials, governors,
and advisers crowded around them and saw that the fire
had not touched them. Not a hair on their heads
was singed, and their clothing was not scorched.
They didn't even smell of smoke!*

—Daniel 3:26–27 NLT

As we saw in the previous reading, there is truly no other god who can rescue like our God. Whatever circumstances you might be thrown into, our Lord Jesus is the fourth man with you *in the midst* of the fire. Notice how He didn't stand outside of the fire, but was in the fire together with the three friends, Shadrach, Meshach, and Abednego.

This brings a whole new meaning for us when we read the verse, "Be strong and of good courage, do not fear nor be afraid of them; for the LORD your God, He *is* the One who **goes with you**. He will not leave you nor forsake you" (Deut. 31:6, boldface mine). Our Lord doesn't deliver you from afar;

He is *with you* in the midst of your adversity. Call upon Him and He will answer you. When Jesus is with you, nothing can harm you!

Don't you just love how the Word of God describes the three friends when they came out of the furnace? They were in the fire, but it had absolutely no power over them. It did not even leave a trace of smoke on them! Now, that's a beautiful picture of God's divine protection!

Beloved, as you call upon the Lord in your day of trouble, my prayer for you is that the trial you are going through will have no power over you; it will not even leave a smell on you. Instead, I declare in Jesus' name that you will walk out of that challenge in your life and the only smell on you will be the fragrance of the Lord Jesus (see 2 Cor. 2:14)! And as the people around you witness how the Lord delivers you, may they come to know His wonderful name and give Him praise. Instead of being negatively affected by whatever trial you might face, I pray that you will receive honor and promotion just like Shadrach, Meshach, and Abednego. Amen!

Today's Prayer

Lord Jesus, thank You that You are always with me and that You will not leave me nor forsake me. Because You are with me, the trial I am going through has no power over me. I declare that because of Your protective covering over me, it will not even leave a trace of smoke on me. Let it instead redound to Your glory and reveal Your power and goodness. Amen.

Today's Thought

The trial I am going through shall not hurt me because the Lord my God goes with me. It will not even leave a trace of smoke on me!

WALK IN WISDOM TO STAY SAFE

*Get wisdom! Get understanding!...Wisdom is
the principal thing; therefore get wisdom. And in
all your getting, get understanding.*

—Proverbs 4:5, 7

It gives me such assurance to know that the Lord can deliver us from trouble. But do you know what's better than being delivered from trouble?

Not *getting* into trouble in the first place.

My dear reader, don't just seek miracles and protection from God without seeking the wisdom from Him to stay protected and out of trouble. There are times when the challenges that we face are beyond our control. But I've found that often, we experience His protection when we follow the Holy Spirit and lean on His wisdom when making decisions. Every day, we need His wisdom, just as we need His protection. After all, Proverbs 4:7 tells us that "wisdom *is* the principal thing," and in all our getting, we need to *get wisdom*.

The Bible tells us that Christ has become for us wisdom

from God (see 1 Cor. 1:30). So what we really need is the Lord
Jesus. We need to lean on Him and draw close to Him daily.
He is our wisdom and only He can cause us to always be at
the right place at the right time. I believe that many troubles
and dangerous situations can be completely avoided when we
don't depend on our own wisdom and planning, but involve
the Lord in all that we do (see Prov. 3:6).

Oftentimes, wisdom and divine protection work hand in
hand. Knowing that we can trust God for His protection certainly does not mean that we should willfully put ourselves in
precarious situations. We need to apply wisdom and heed the
Lord's leading through the wise counsel of the people around
us, such as our leaders in the local church and our spouses.
Proverbs 11:14 tells us, "Where *there is* no counsel, the people
fall; but in the multitude of counselors *there is* safety." For
instance, if your spouse has been telling you that you have a
problem with speeding, please take heed.

While there can be divine protection, do not be foolish
and think that you can do whatever you want and nothing
untoward will ever happen to you. I pray that as you involve
the Lord and learn to walk in wisdom, you'll begin to walk in
a greater measure of peace, protection, and good success.

Today's Prayer

*Heavenly Father, thank You that I can come to You and
receive wisdom to walk in safety. Thank You that Jesus
has become wisdom for me and will lead and guide me
in all that I need to do. Help me also to apply wisdom
and heed Your leading through the wise counsel
of the people around me. Amen.*

Today's Thought

*I need God's wisdom, just as I need His protection.
Jesus is my wisdom and I look to Him to lead
and guide me in all that I do.*

DISCERNMENT
AND WISDOM

*Be very careful, then, how you live—not as unwise
but as wise, making the most of every opportunity,
because the days are evil. Therefore do not be foolish,
but understand what the Lord's will is.*

—Ephesians 5:15–17 NIV

❧

In the previous reading, we talked about how we stay safe and protected when we don't act presumptuously or irresponsibly but lean in to God's wisdom. The Lord Jesus demonstrated this to us Himself. When the devil tried to tempt Him to jump off the pinnacle of the temple, quoting Scripture to say that angels were supposed to bear Him up, our Lord Jesus responded by saying, "The Scriptures also say, 'You must not test the LORD your God'" (Matt. 4:7 NLT). Likewise, let us not test the Lord by making irresponsible and unwise decisions that ignore the written Word of God or the godly counsel spoken over our lives.

When you are led by His wisdom, the Lord can protect you from making unwise decisions. For example, someone may offer you "the investment opportunity of a lifetime." On the surface, everything might seem to check out and it may appear to be a legitimate opportunity that is not to be missed. But before you rush to commit to anything, can I encourage you to first ask the Lord for His wisdom and leading?

There is a principle we can learn from in Isaiah 11, where it says of the Lord that "the spirit of wisdom and understanding" will rest on Him, and "He will not judge by what His eyes see, nor make a decision by what His ears hear" (Isa. 11:2–3 NASB). You see, there is a discernment and wisdom from the Lord that goes beyond looking at the outward appearance of a matter. When you call on Him, He will answer you and give you an answer of peace. If you don't feel a peace to proceed, don't allow anyone to pressure you into making a decision you will regret!

Today's Prayer

Lord Jesus, thank You for giving me discernment and wisdom to help me make wise decisions. Thank You that Your Spirit helps me see beyond outward appearances and leads me to do what is truly best for me. I believe that when I call on You, You will answer me and give me an answer of peace. Amen.

Today's Thought

The Lord gives me discernment and wisdom to help me see beyond outward appearances. When I call on Him, He will lead me with peace.

DAY 7

BE LED BY THE
HOLY SPIRIT

*Now when they had gone through Phrygia and
the region of Galatia, they were forbidden by the
Holy Spirit to preach the word in Asia. After they had
come to Mysia, they tried to go into Bithynia,
but the Spirit did not permit them.*

—Acts 16:6–7

The more areas of your life you involve the Lord in, the more you can experience His protection. You can even ask the Lord to guide you in something as seemingly natural as your travel itinerary. In fact, read the passage above. The apostle Paul allowed the Holy Spirit to lead them at every step.

We see from those Scriptures that closed doors are not necessarily negative, and could be signs of God's protection over our lives. The challenge for some of us is that we are so adept at planning and scheduling our busy lives that many times, we don't make room for the Lord to intervene and to guide us to be at the right place at the right time. Let's not put our trust in our intelligence and planning, but in His wisdom, leading, and counsel. There is a proverb that says, "A man's heart plans his way, but the LORD directs his steps" (Prov. 16:9). Even as we plan, I pray that we will always remember to commit all our ways to the Lord, and allow *Him* to direct our steps.

Being led by the Spirit does not have to be something complicated. When you walk close to the Lord and have a close relationship with Him, He can lead you in supernaturally natural ways. Some years ago, a couple in our church were vacationing at a beach resort on Penang Island in Malaysia, when the wife felt like eating something in another location on the mainland. Because of that "prompting" in her belly, they headed off earlier than they had originally planned. While they were loading their vehicle, a man kept hurrying them and asking them to move off as they were apparently blocking the hotel driveway, and that had really irritated them at that time.

In any case, just fifteen minutes after they had crossed from the island to the mainland, they heard the news that an earthquake in the Indian Ocean had triggered a killer tsunami that crashed onto the beachfront they were at, killing more than fifty people. Had they left just a little later, they could have been among the casualties of the tragedy that day. Looking back, the couple believes that the man at the hotel might even have been an angel sent by the Lord to get them out of harm's way quickly.

I don't know about you, but I want the Lord to direct *all* my steps! Call upon Him today and He will answer you.

———

Today's Prayer
Lord Jesus, thank You that I can commit all my ways to You and allow You to direct my steps. Thank You that being led by the Spirit does not have to be complicated. I believe that as I walk close to You, You are leading me every day in supernaturally natural ways. Amen.

Today's Thought
Being led by the Spirit does not have to be complicated. When I walk close to the Lord, He will lead me in supernaturally natural ways.

SECTION XII

GOD'S PROMISE OF LONG LIFE

*"With long life I will satisfy him,
And show him My salvation."*

—*Psalm 91:16*

DAY 1

HE SATISFIES YOU
WITH LONG LIFE

"With long life I will satisfy him, and show him
My salvation."

—Psalm 91:16

We have come to the final but, I think, most important verse in Psalm 91! If you ever had any doubt that God desires for you to live a long, good life, let this verse be your answer. You may be battling with a health condition right now, but by faith let's hold fast to this verse together. In Jesus' mighty name, I see you healed, healthy, and whole. I see you strong in Christ and ready to take on any giant that is ahead of you.

One of my favorite pictures of long life is found in the biblical character Caleb. When he was eighty-five years old, he said, "I am this day, eighty-five years old. As yet I *am as* strong this day as on the day that Moses sent me; just as my strength *was* then, so now *is* my strength for war" (Josh. 14:10–11). The faith picture here of long life is not just in terms of *quantity*—the number of days—but also *quality*—health and strength. Caleb remained as strong at eighty-five as he was when he was forty-five. Which means in the last forty years in the harsh wilderness, his strength, youth, and vigor didn't diminish. There was no leaking, no receding, and no fading away of his strength!

If perhaps you think that Caleb was just talking big, look at what he said next: "Now therefore, give me this mountain of which the LORD spoke in that day; for you heard in that day how the Anakim *were* there, and *that* the cities *were* great *and* fortified. It may be that the LORD *will be* with me, and I shall be able to drive them out as the LORD said" (Josh. 14:12).

At eighty-five, Caleb was ready to fight with *giants* to gain possession of a mountain! And Caleb did as he said! Read the evidence for yourself: "Hebron therefore became the inheritance of Caleb the son of Jephunneh the Kenizzite to this day, because he wholly followed the LORD God of Israel" (Josh. 14:14).

You were impressed when a teenage shepherd boy picked a fight with one giant named Goliath? We should be completely blown away by this eighty-five-year-old, who took on a *whole mountain* packed with giants! Caleb was zealous for the Lord's glory. As far as he was concerned, there was unfinished business because the Lord had promised them the mountain forty years ago. My personal belief is that his biological clock stopped ticking and he basically stopped aging because he kept his eyes not on himself, but on the promises of the Lord. As you meditate on and find strength in God's promises, the same can happen for you!

Today's Prayer

Dear Father in heaven, thank You that one of Your desires is for me to have a long, healthy, strong life that is truly satisfying. Thank You that You renew my youth and strength. I declare that because of Your Word and presence in my life, I remain strong to take on any giant that is ahead of me. Amen.

Today's Thought

A long, healthy, strong life that is truly satisfying is God's desire for me.

FOLLOW THE LORD

*Hebron therefore became the inheritance of Caleb…because he **wholly followed** the* LORD *God of Israel.*

—*Joshua 14:14 (boldface mine)*

⌇

What are your eyes fixed on today? Are they focused on the darkness that is in the world? Or are they fixed on the Lord's promises for your life? My chief intention in this book has been to turn your eyes away from the destruction you see every day, and to turn them to our beautiful Lord Jesus.

Do you know what Caleb's secret to long life was? The passage above tells us that it was found in simply *following* the Lord. Hebron was the name for one of the cities of refuge we talked about in section 7. In Hebrew, "Hebron" means fellowship or association. This speaks of intimacy, closeness, and connection with the Lord.

There is no formula to long life. The prayer of protection is not a mantra. What we have been talking about throughout this book all point back to the importance of having an intimate relationship with Jesus. Our Lord Jesus is the way, the truth, and the life. He came that we might have life and have it more abundantly. *Follow* Him and find the path to a long and abundant life. Don't forget that everything Caleb experienced was under the old covenant. His renewal of youth and unabated strength and vigor were all experienced under the old covenant. *How much more* should we be experiencing this renewal of youth, boundless energy, and length of days under the new covenant of grace that is established on better promises (see Heb. 8:6)! Amen!

In a psalm that Moses wrote, it says, "The days of our lives *are* seventy years; and if by reason of strength *they are* eighty years" (Ps. 90:10). Some people have used this to teach that our expected lifespan is therefore between seventy and eighty years. But it is important we interpret this psalm in the context of the children of Israel being in the wilderness and under God's wrath. We have also seen that even under the old covenant, Caleb transcended this lifespan and was still going strong at eighty-five years old.

So dear reader—you who are under the new covenant—I encourage you to aim high. Don't settle for living till just seventy or eighty years old, when God has promised, "With long life I will **satisfy him**, and show him My salvation" (Ps. 91:16, boldface mine). *Your satisfaction* is the limit and according to your faith, be it unto you. I pray that as you stay close to our

Lord Jesus, you will live long, live strong, and live under the protective covering of His wings.

––––––––

Today's Prayer

Lord Jesus, thank You that You are the way, the truth, and the life. Thank You that You came that I might have life and have it abundantly. I believe that as I follow You, You will keep me and give me a life full of good days. I will enjoy a long and satisfying life under the protective covering of Your wings. Amen.

Today's Thought

Jesus came that I might have life and have it abundantly. As I follow and stay close to Him, He will cause me to live a long and satisfying life under the protective covering of His wings.

SALVATION IN THE NAME OF JESUS

*And the Lord will deliver me from **every evil work** and preserve me for His heavenly kingdom.*

—*2 Timothy 4:18 (boldface mine)*

Psalm 91 ends with the power-packed verse, "With long life I will satisfy him, and show him My salvation." Many years ago, the Lord opened my eyes to see that apart from the four names of God that we covered in the first two verses of Psalm 91, there is another name of God, a fifth name, concealed in the very last word of Psalm 91.

You see, in Hebrew, the word "salvation" is the word *yeshua*.[26] And *Yeshua* is the Hebrew name of our Lord Jesus! Now, isn't that beautiful? This is what God was saying: "With long life I will satisfy him, and show him My *Yeshua*." Long life is found in our *Yeshua*. You can know God as *El Elyon*, God Most High, as the Almighty *Shaddai*, as *Jehovah*, and even as *Elohim*, but the name that gives you full and utter confidence is the name Jesus!

It is not enough to know that God is all-powerful. It is

more important you know that God is willing to use His power and might to *save you*! That's what our Lord Jesus did at the cross for you and me. He came and He showed us His salvation by sacrificing Himself on the cross for your sins and my sins. *He died young that we may live long.* And not just live long in this world. At the cross, He purchased for us the gift of eternal life, paid for with His own blood. The moment you received Jesus as your Lord and Savior, your salvation in Him was sure and secure!

I grew up in a church where I was taught that when you sin, you will lose your salvation and have to get born again all over again. This erroneous teaching oppressed my mind day and night. The enemy incessantly attacked me with thoughts that I had lost my salvation. As I was seeking the Lord for answers one day, He opened my eyes and pointed me to the above Scripture passage from 2 Timothy.

Just like that, when the truth of God's Word came in, all the oppression left me. And every time the thought that I had lost my salvation reared its ugly head again, I would quote this verse, boldly declaring, "It is written, 'And the Lord will deliver me from every evil work and preserve me for His heavenly kingdom.'" Beloved, I highly recommend that you meditate on this Scripture. In this one verse you find the Lord's protection and preservation unto eternity!

Today's Prayer

Beloved Lord Jesus, thank You that You are my Yeshua, my sure salvation. Thank You that You purchased the gift of eternal life for me with Your own blood. I believe and declare that You will deliver me from every evil work and preserve me for Your heavenly kingdom. Amen.

Today's Thought

My Yeshua, the Lord Jesus, purchased the gift of eternal life for me. He will surely deliver me from every evil work and preserve me for His heavenly kingdom.

WORSHIP THE LORD

Oh come, let us worship and bow down; let us kneel
before the LORD our Maker. For He is our God, and we
are the people of His pasture, and the sheep of His hand.
—Psalm 95:6–7

I am sure that you have heard a lot of teaching on fearing the Lord. I do believe in a reverential honor of the Lord. But I am not for any kind of teaching that promotes this idea that God wants you to be afraid of Him. Throughout this entire book, I have shown you how much God delights in having us *close* to Him. He welcomes us to dwell in His secret place, to be so close to Him that we come under His shadow. These are all pictures of intimacy. In any relationship, fear and intimacy cannot coexist. If you fear God today, you won't be able to believe Him for His protection. That is why it is so important for you to be strong and established in His grace.

The author of the book of Hebrews says, "Let us therefore come boldly to the throne of grace, that we may obtain mercy and find grace to help in time of need" (Heb. 4:16). This is a picture of the ark of the covenant (which we covered in section 4), God's throne of grace. Because our Lord's blood has been shed on the mercy seat, today, we can come boldly into His presence without any sense of inferiority or shame, and receive His favor, His supply, His protection, and His help in our time of need.

Jesus defined the fear of the Lord as the *worship* of the Lord. (I touched on this in section 8.) In the wilderness temptation, Jesus responded to the devil by saying, "Away with you, Satan! For it is written, 'You shall worship the LORD your God, and Him only you shall serve" (Matt. 4:8–10). Our Lord was quoting from Deuteronomy 6:13, which says, "You shall fear the LORD your God and serve Him." Our Lord substituted the word "fear" with the word "worship."

Jesus was showing us how to accurately understand the fear of the Lord. In the new covenant, it has nothing to do with being afraid of the Lord; it has everything to do with coming into His presence with boldness and worshiping Him. Stop living in fear, my friend. Instead, follow our Lord wholly like Caleb did and worship His wonderful name. The prayer of protection is a psalm of worship. When you worship Jesus, all your fears will fade away. When you worship Him, the angel of the Lord encamps around you like a shield of protection. When you worship your Savior, His Spirit of wisdom and counsel will lead and guide you with rivers of peace!

Today's Prayer

*Father God, I come and worship and bow down before You
without shame or fear. Thank You that because of Jesus'
shed blood I can always come boldly before the throne of
grace and receive Your favor and protection. I worship Your
wonderful name and set my heart to follow You. Amen.*

Today's Thought

*Fearing the Lord has nothing to do with being afraid of
Him, but everything to do with coming into His presence
with boldness and worshiping Him.*

THE LORD WILL LEAD
AND GUIDE YOU

"The LORD will guide you continually, giving you water
when you are dry and restoring your strength. You will be
like a well-watered garden, like an ever-flowing spring."
—Isaiah 58:11 NLT

A lady from Virginia wrote to share with me her testimony of how following the leading of the Lord guided and protected her and her daughters. Be blessed as you see how practical the Lord was in looking after all their needs and keeping them safe:

In one of your messages of the year, you mentioned that we needed the Lord's protection. I listened to that message over and over again, and confessed that we were crowned with the Lord's glory and honor.

In April, a few days before my two daughters and I left for a road trip, I had the urge to read Psalm 91 and Psalm 23 with my children. We read the Scriptures and quoted verses out loud, and then I read it again to my girls as they drifted off to sleep.

On the day of the trip, we encountered horrendous storms with awfully dark clouds, torrential winds, and hail as we drove through Virginia and Tennessee. In my heart, I felt that I needed to just drive through the storms and did so by God's grace. We stopped to eat in north Georgia. I wanted to hurry and eat so that we could get back on the road quickly. But in my heart, I felt the Lord telling me to slow down and not to rush my girls.

When we left the restaurant, I felt the urge to get gas at the gas station next door. I didn't know why because my gas tank was already more than half full. But I did it anyway. Then, we got back on the highway and continued our trip.

After traveling less than a mile, the traffic came to a complete stop. We waited for a while and then realized that a large tornado had just torn through the town directly in front of us only minutes before! It had caused destruction on the very section of the highway that we were going to travel on. By God's grace, He had slowed us down enough to keep us from the destructive tornado by three to five minutes!

We were stuck on the highway for five hours as emergency crews helped the victims of the tornado. We prayed in the Spirit for the victims and sang praises to the Lord for His saving grace. Although we couldn't move for five hours, we now had enough gas in our car to keep the DVD playing (for the girls) for most of the five hours. The Lord had prepared us for this without me even knowing it.

While we waited, another storm traveled over us. It shook our SUV violently and the radio warned that another tornado was imminent. We were stuck on the highway with no way to exit. I began to confess Psalm 91 over us and told my daughters that the Lord would keep us safe no matter what the storm looked like. The Word of God calmed our hearts. We turned off the bad news on the radio and just sang praises to God for His protection. Amazingly, the second storm didn't produce another tornado! The Lord kept us safe and I am so thankful!

The devil intended to cause destruction in our lives but the Lord's amazing power, love, and grace made sure that we were always held safe and warm in the secret place of the Most High.

Thank you so much for preaching the true gospel of Jesus Christ. God bless and keep you and your family!

Don't you just love how the Lord led this family in such specific ways by getting them to read the psalm of protection, stay longer at that restaurant, and even to top up on gas? When we follow Him and allow Him to lead us, the Lord Jesus—our salvation—saves us!

Today's Prayer
Lord Jesus, thank You for Your promise to lead and guide me continually. Thank You that as I worship You, all my fears fade away and You keep me safe and warm in Your secret place. I believe that Your Spirit of wisdom will guide me with peace and provide for all my needs. Amen.

Today's Thought
When I worship the Lord, all my fears fade away and His Spirit will lead and guide me continually.

COME BOLDLY INTO JESUS' PRESENCE

*"On that day I will raise up the tabernacle
of David, which has fallen down, and repair its
damages; I will raise up its ruins, and rebuild
it as in the days of old."*

—*Amos 9:11*

The prophetic passage above speaks of our time. The interesting feature about the tabernacle of David in contrast to the tabernacle of Moses is that it had no veil separating man and God. David could go directly to worship the Lord before the ark of the covenant.

When our Lord Jesus died on the cross and cried out, "It is finished!" (John 19:30), the Bible tells us that at that precise moment "the veil of the temple was torn in two from top to bottom" (Matt. 27:51), opening the way into the Holy of Holies! Through Christ, there is no longer any separation between God and man. *Whosoever* believes in Jesus shall never perish. Hallelujah!

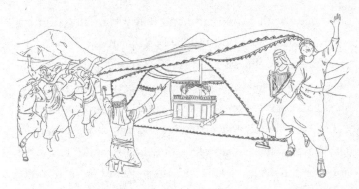

David's tabernacle: David and the priests could praise God openly before the ark of the covenant.

Isn't it wonderful to know that when you are in Christ, all your sins are forgiven, and that you can come boldly to His throne of grace to worship Him? God has raised up the tabernacle of David with a new generation of worshipers who are not afraid of God and not afraid to draw near and receive His promise of divine protection. None of us can ever do enough to merit God's protection, but praise be to God, we are all qualified by the blood of Jesus Christ!

On the night of the first Passover, when the children of Israel applied the blood of an innocent lamb on their doorposts, God said to them, "Now the blood shall be a sign for you on the houses where you *are*. And when I see the blood, I will pass over you; and the plague shall not be on you to destroy *you* when I strike the land of Egypt" (Exod. 12:13).

Jesus became that innocent lamb that was sacrificed for us when He shed His blood and died on the cross.

Today, as believers in Christ, His blood protects us. I'm believing with you that all evil, all destruction, and all danger shall pass over you and not come near you and your family. Let us come boldly to worship our Lord in the tabernacle of David where there is no veil. Come boldly under His wings and worship the Lord daily with the prayer of protection. His precious blood has been shed at the mercy seat for our total redemption, protection, and salvation.

Psalm 91 was written for worship. Come boldly into our Lord's presence daily and pray the prayer of protection. There is no veil, no failure, and no shame that separates you from God today because of our Lord's finished work at Calvary. Come before your heavenly Father, worship Him, and receive His protection for you and your entire household!

Today's Prayer
*Heavenly Father, thank You that because of Jesus' perfect
work on the cross, there is no longer any separation
between me and You. Thank You that I can come boldly
into Your presence and worship You. I believe that all evil,
all destruction, and all danger shall pass over me and
not come near me and my family. Amen.*

Today's Thought
*Because the blood of Christ protects me, all evil,
all destruction, and all danger shall pass over me and
not come near me and my family.*

DAY 7

LIVE IN THE SHADOW
OF HIS WINGS

*My soul trusts in You; and in the shadow of
Your wings I will make my refuge, until these
calamities have passed by.*

—*Psalm 57:1*

While it's true that we live in dangerous times, I want you to know this: We have our Abba's promise that we can live safe, secure, and protected no matter what turmoil may be around us. Our heavenly Father does not want His children partaking of the fear that has invaded the hearts of people of the world. In fact, He wants *every* trace of fear to be expelled from your heart, knowing that He has set you apart, and that He who watches over you *never* slumbers nor sleeps! When fear comes knocking, let God's promises of protection fill your heart, mind, and mouth, and the God of peace, our *Jehovah Shalom*, will come into and move in your situation!

Our Lord Jesus desires to have an intimate relationship with us and He loves it when we acknowledge our need for Him. He loves it when we allow Him to hide us under the shadow of His wings, close to His heart of love. The prayer of protection is not some magical chant or incantation that grants us protection. Our protection in the Lord is all about us being intimate with and close to Him. As you involve Him in your day-to-day life, you will see Him lead you by His wisdom and protect you from making unwise decisions. And I pray that you will see His protection manifested more and more as you grow in your revelation of how deeply loved you are by the Lord, who protects like no other.

I am so grateful to the precious people who took the time to write to me to share the amazing stories you've read here. I hope these encounters with real people around the world have encouraged you to believe that whatever weapon the enemy may have fashioned against you, it will *not* prosper. God is no respecter of persons—as you keep establishing your heart on the word of grace, as you keep hearing testimonies of His goodness, *you* will also experience miracles of deliverance, protection, and healing in your life.

Today, as you put your trust in the Lord, I pray that you will experience not just His divine protection in a greater measure, but *every* blessing that the Lord Jesus has purchased for you on the cross of Calvary. Beloved, as we garrison our hearts with the truths and promises of Psalm 91, I pray that we will truly live confidently and fearlessly in these dangerous times.

Today's Prayer

Lord Jesus, thank You that as I live in the shadow of Your wings, close to Your heart, every trace of fear is being expelled from my heart. Thank You that the truths and promises of Psalm 91 garrison my heart and mind against all anxieties. I declare that because of Your love for me, I can live fearlessly in these dangerous times. Amen.

Today's Thought

When I allow God's promises of protection to fill my heart, mind, and mouth, I will truly live confidently and fearlessly and experience miracles of deliverance, protection, and healing in my life.

NOTES

[1] OT: 3427, James Strong, *Biblesoft's New Exhaustive Strong's Numbers and Concordance with Expanded Greek-Hebrew Dictionary*. Copyright © 1994, 2003, 2006 Biblesoft, Inc. and International Bible Translators, Inc.

[2] OT: 4268, Joseph Henry Thayer, Francis Brown, Samuel Rolles Driver, and Charles Augustus Briggs, *The Online Bible Thayer's Greek Lexicon and Brown Driver & Briggs Hebrew Lexicon*. Copyright © 1993, Woodside Bible Fellowship, Ontario, Canada. Licensed from the Institute for Creation Research.

[3] OT: 4686, James Strong, *Biblesoft's New Exhaustive Strong's Numbers and Concordance with Expanded Greek-Hebrew Dictionary*. Copyright © 1994, 2003, 2006 Biblesoft, Inc. and International Bible Translators, Inc.

[4] OT: 3068, William Edwy Vine, *Vine's Expository Dictionary of Biblical Words*. Copyright © 1985, Thomas Nelson Publishers.

[5] Retrieved March 24, 2016, from www.hebrew-streams.org/frontstuff/jesus-yeshua.html

[6] Retrieved March 24, 2016, from www.hebrew4christians.com/Names_of_G-d/Elohim/elohim.html

[7] OT: 6256, William Edwy Vine, *Vine's Expository Dictionary of Biblical Words*. Copyright © 1985, Thomas Nelson Publishers.

[8] OT: 6293, James Strong, *Biblesoft's New Exhaustive Strong's Numbers and Concordance with Expanded Greek-Hebrew Dictionary*. Copyright © 1994, 2003, 2006 Biblesoft, Inc. and International Bible Translators, Inc.

[9] OT: 4745, James Strong, *Biblesoft's New Exhaustive Strong's Numbers and Concordance with Expanded Greek-Hebrew Dictionary*. Copyright © 1994, 2003, 2006 Biblesoft, Inc. and International Bible Translators, Inc.

[10] OT: 3727, William Edwy Vine, *Vine's Expository Dictionary of Biblical Words*. Copyright © 1985, Thomas Nelson Publishers.

[11] NT: 2799, James Strong, *Biblesoft's New Exhaustive Strong's Numbers and Concordance with Expanded Greek-Hebrew Dictionary*. Copyright © 1994, 2003, 2006 Biblesoft, Inc. and International Bible Translators, Inc.

[12] Retrieved March 31, 2016, from www.blueletterbible.org/lang/Lexicon/lexicon.cfm?strongs=H7965&t=KJV.

[13] Retrieved April 1, 2016, from http://eresources.nlb.gov.sg/infopedia/articles/SIP_1529_2009-06-03.html.

[14] Retrieved April 7, 2016, from www.biblestudytools.com/dictionaries/smiths-bible-dictionary/kedesh.html.

[15] Retrieved April 7, 2016, from www.biblestudytools.com/dictionaries/smiths-bible-dictionary/shechem.html.

[16] Retrieved April 7, 2016, from http://biblehub.com/topical/h/hebron.htm.

[17] OT: 1221, Joseph Henry Thayer, Francis Brown, Samuel Rolles Driver, and Charles Augustus Briggs, *The Online Bible Thayer's Greek Lexicon and Brown Driver & Briggs Hebrew Lexicon*. Copyright © 1993, Woodside Bible Fellowship, Ontario, Canada. Licensed from the Institute for Creation Research.

[18] OT: 7216, Joseph Henry Thayer, Francis Brown, Samuel Rolles Driver, and Charles Augustus Briggs, *The Online Bible Thayer's Greek Lexicon and Brown Driver & Briggs Hebrew Lexicon*. Copyright © 1993, Woodside Bible Fellowship, Ontario, Canada. Licensed from the Institute for Creation Research.

[19] OT: 1474, Joseph Henry Thayer, Francis Brown, Samuel Rolles Driver, and Charles Augustus Briggs, *The Online Bible Thayer's Greek Lexicon and Brown Driver & Briggs Hebrew Lexicon*. Copyright © 1993, Woodside Bible Fellowship, Ontario, Canada. Licensed from the Institute for Creation Research.

[20] OT: 2620, James Strong, *Biblesoft's New Exhaustive Strong's Numbers and Concordance with Expanded Greek-Hebrew Dictionary*. Copyright © 1994, 2003, 2006 Biblesoft, Inc. and International Bible Translators, Inc.

[21] OT: 1870, Joseph Henry Thayer, Francis Brown, Samuel Rolles Driver, and Charles Augustus Briggs, *The Online Bible Thayer's Greek Lexicon and Brown Driver & Briggs Hebrew Lexicon*. Copyright © 1993, Woodside Bible Fellowship, Ontario, Canada. Licensed from the Institute for Creation Research.

[22] OT: 7522, Joseph Henry Thayer, Francis Brown, Samuel Rolles Driver, and Charles Augustus Briggs, *The Online Bible Thayer's Greek Lexicon and Brown Driver & Briggs Hebrew Lexicon*. Copyright © 1993, Woodside Bible Fellowship, Ontario, Canada. Licensed from the Institute for Creation Research.

[23] OT: 3722, Joseph Henry Thayer, Francis Brown, Samuel Rolles Driver, and Charles Augustus Briggs, *The Online Bible Thayer's Greek Lexicon and Brown Driver & Briggs Hebrew Lexicon*. Copyright © 1993, Woodside Bible Fellowship, Ontario, Canada. Licensed from the Institute for Creation Research.

[24] Retrieved, April 14, 2016, from www.blueletterbible.org/lang/lexicon/lexicon.cfm?t=kjv&strongs=g5083.

[25] OT: 1657, Joseph Henry Thayer, Francis Brown, Samuel Rolles Driver, and Charles Augustus Briggs, *The Online Bible Thayer's Greek Lexicon and Brown Driver & Briggs Hebrew Lexicon*. Copyright © 1993, Woodside Bible Fellowship, Ontario, Canada. Licensed from the Institute for Creation Research.

[26] OT: 3444, Joseph Henry Thayer, Francis Brown, Samuel Rolles Driver, and Charles Augustus Briggs, *The Online Bible Thayer's Greek Lexicon and Brown Driver & Briggs Hebrew Lexicon*. Copyright © 1993, Woodside Bible Fellowship, Ontario, Canada. Licensed from the Institute for Creation Research.

SALVATION PRAYER

If you would like to receive all that Jesus has done for you and make Him your Lord and Savior, please pray this prayer:

Lord Jesus, thank You for loving me and dying for me on the cross. Your precious blood washes me clean of every sin. You are my Lord and my Savior, now and for-ever. I believe You rose from the dead and that You are alive today. Because of Your finished work, I am now a beloved child of God and heaven is my home. Thank You for giving me eternal life and filling my heart with Your peace and joy. Amen.

WE WOULD LIKE TO HEAR FROM YOU

If you have prayed the salvation prayer or if you have a testimony to share after reading this book, please tell us about it via JosephPrince.com/testimony.

STAY CONNECTED
WITH JOSEPH

⁓⁂⁓

Connect with Joseph through these social media channels and receive daily inspirational teachings:

Facebook.com/JosephPrince
Twitter.com/JosephPrince
Youtube.com/JosephPrinceOnline
Instagram: @JosephPrince

FREE DAILY E-MAIL
DEVOTIONAL

⁓⁂⁓

Sign up for Joseph's FREE daily e-mail devotional at JosephPrince.com/meditate and receive bite-size inspirations to help you grow in grace.

BOOKS BY JOSEPH PRINCE

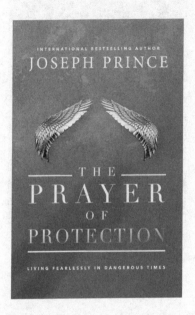

The Prayer of Protection

We live in dangerous times. A time in which terrorist activities, pandemics, and natural calamities are on the rise. But there is good news. God has given us a powerful prayer of protection—Psalm 91—through which we and our families can find safety and deliverance from every snare of the enemy. In *The Prayer of Protection*, discover a God of love and His impenetrable shield of protection that covers everything that concerns you, and start living fearlessly in these dangerous times!

Grace Revolution

Experience the revolution that is sweeping across the world! In *Grace Revolution*, Joseph Prince offers five powerful keys that will help you experience firsthand the grace revolution in your own life, and live above defeat. See how these keys can work easily for you, as you read inspiring stories of people who experienced amazing and lasting transformations when they encountered the real Jesus and heard the unadulterated gospel. Whatever your challenge today, begin to step away from defeat and take a massive leap toward your victory. Get your copy today and let the revolution begin in your life!

The Power of Right Believing

Experience transformation, breakthroughs, and freedom today through the power of right believing! This book offers seven practical and powerful keys that will help you find freedom from all fears, guilt, and addictions. See these keys come alive in the many precious testimonies you will read from people around the world who have experienced breakthroughs and liberty from all kinds of bondages. Win the battle for your mind through understanding the powerful truths of God's Word and begin a journey of victorious living and unshakable confidence in God's love for you!

Destined to Reign

This pivotal and quintessential book on the grace of God will change your life forever! Join Joseph Prince as he unlocks foundational truths to understanding God's grace and how it alone sets you free to experience victory over every adversity, lack, and destructive habit that is limiting you today. Be uplifted and refreshed as you discover how reigning in life is all about Jesus and what He has already done for you. Start experiencing the success, wholeness, and victory that you were destined to enjoy!

Unmerited Favor

This follow-up book to *Destined To Reign* is a must-read if you want to live out the dreams that God has birthed in your heart! Building on the foundational truths of God's grace laid out in *Destined To Reign*, *Unmerited Favor* takes you into a deeper understanding of the gift of righteousness that you have through the cross and how it gives you a supernatural ability to succeed in life. Packed with empowering new covenant truths, *Unmerited Favor* will set you free to soar above your challenges and lead an overcoming life as God's beloved today.

REFLECTIONS

REFLECTIONS

REFLECTIONS